The Canadian Spelling Program 2.1

5

Ruth Scott

Sharon Siamon

gage EDUCATIONAL PUBLISHING COMPANY
A DIVISION OF CANADA PUBLISHING CORPORATION
Vancouver · Calgary · Toronto · London · H

Canadian Cataloguing in Publication Data

Scott, Ruth, 1949
The Canadian spelling program 2.1, 5
ISBN 0-7715-1582-0
1. Spellers. 2. English language - Orthography and spelling - Problems, exercises, etc. I. Siamon, Sharon. II. Title.
PE1145.2.S37 1996   428.1   C95-932182-9

Design: Pronk&Associates

Illustration: Graham Bardell, Graham Pilsworth, Barbara Reid

Cover Photograph: Dave Starrett

The authors and publisher gratefully acknowledge the contributions of the following educators to *The Canadian Spelling Program 2.1*:

Lynn Archer
Surrey, British Columbia

Judith MacManus
Riverview, New Brunswick

Sylvia Arnold
Aurora, Ontario

Denis Maika
Mississauga, Ontario

Carol Chandler
Halifax, Nova Scotia

Bill Nimigon
North York, Ontario

Linda Hollowell
North York, Ontario

Gordon Williamson
Winnipeg, Manitoba

Caroline Lutyk
Burlington, Ontario

ISBN 0-7715-**1582-0**

 2 3 4 5 BP 00 99 98 97 96

Written, Printed, and Bound in Canada

CONTENTS

▼▼▼

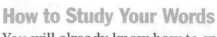

How to Study Your Words

You will already know how to spell some of the words in this book, but there might be some words that are hard for you.

When you need to study a word, use these steps:
1. **Look** at the word, letter by letter.
2. **Say** the word to yourself, listening carefully.
3. **Cover** the word.
4. **Write** the word.
5. **Check** the spelling, letter by letter, with the word in the list.

If you make a mistake, notice where it is. Did you make a mistake at the beginning of the word, or in the middle, or at the end? Was your mistake with a consonant letter, or a vowel letter, or both?

Now do all the steps over again with the same word.

Dictionary Symbols

Look at these symbols: /**a**/ /**ē**/ /**är**/ /**k**/.

Symbols like these stand for sounds. For example, the symbol /a/ stands for the short vowel **a** you hear at the beginning of **a**pple. You will find these symbols in the dictionary and other books about words.

New Words

The new words in this spelling book may come from the areas of technology, from culture, or they may simply be old words with new meanings. You will probably find many others you can add to the list.

Preferred Spelling

You will notice that some words spelled with **or** in the first edition of this book (**color**, **favorite**, **neighbor**) are spelled **our** in this revised edition (**colour**, **favourite**, **neighbour**). The **our** spelling is now considered the preferred Canadian spelling.

Long a
a_e ay ai
base   display   trail

understand
tracked
female
chase
stayed
anyway
display
remain
fail
male
trail
attack
base
capture
valleys
gorilla

Exploring the World of a Shy Giant

The rare mountain gorilla lives on the slopes of the Virungu Volcanoes in East Africa. From a base camp at the foot of the mountains, the gorilla bands are tracked by guides who understand their habits. The gorillas leave a trail of broken plants up the steep-sided valleys. At some points leaves and branches mark where they stayed for the night. The male gorillas have a mass of up to 200 kilograms, the female about half of that. The head male will chase and attack any intruder who gives a display of anger. If a visitor can remain quiet and still, gorillas are quite tame and shy. Some people have tried to capture baby gorillas for zoos. But gorillas will fight to the death to defend their young. Since the young animals fail to survive in zoos anyway, this is a cruel practice. Money from tourists who want to visit gorillas in the wild is now helping to save them from extinction.

Observing Patterns

1. Write the three list words that contain double consonants.

2. Write the two list words that mean actions that were completed in the past. Underline the base word for each.

3. Write the three list words that have three syllables.

4. Unscramble the pair of rhyming list words in each cave.

liart
afil

splayid
yanyaw

sabe
sahec

5. Write the list word that means the opposite of each word below.

succeed   male   release   leave

Discovering Patterns

understand tracked female chase stayed anyway display remain fail male trail attack base capture valleys gorilla

1. Write the list words that have the short sound /a/ as in **tack**. Circle the letter that makes this sound.

2. Make a chart in your notebook like the one below. Write the following list words under the correct headings.

female   chase   stayed   remain

display   fail   male   trail   base

long **a** spelled **ay** as in **day**	long **a** spelled **ai** as in **sail**	long **a** spelled **a_e** as in **name**

POWERBOOSTER

- The short vowel sound /a/ is usually spelled **a** as in **capture**.
- The long vowel sound /ā/ may be spelled **ay** as in **stayed**, **ai** as in **fail**, or **a_e** as in **base**.

Exploring Patterns

1. Climb the mountain! As you meet each letter, make a word that rhymes with **fail**. The answers all contain /ā/ spelled **ai**.

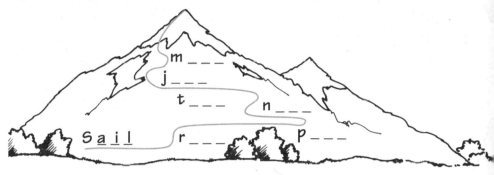

m _ _ _
j _ _ _
t _ _ _   n _ _ _
S a i l   r _ _ _   p _ _ _

2. Write the words that fit these clues! The answers are all words that end in **-ture**, as in **capture**.

    a) _ _ _ ture   a drawing or photograph
    b) _ _ _ _ _ ture   an exciting or dangerous experience
    c) _ _ _ ture   a bird that eats dead animals
    d) _ _ ture   the world not made by humans

3. Follow the trail of gorilla tracks. Write the word from each pair of prints that has the /a/ sound as in **valley**.

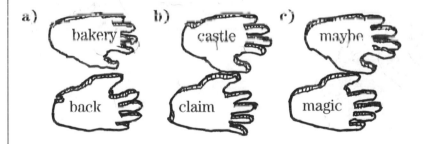

a) bakery / back   b) castle / claim   c) maybe / magic

4. The dictionary gives a number of meanings for the word **base**. Read the entry below.

> **base** (bās) **1** the part of a thing on which it rests; bottom
> **2** in certain games, a station or goal **3** a starting place
> **4** a permanent camp or other place where units of the armed forces are stationed.

Write the number of the definition that fits the meaning of **base** in each of the sentences below.

    a) The player slid into third base.
    b) There is an armed forces base at Gagetown.
    c) The machine rests on a steel base.
    d) The base of our hiking trip was beside a brook.

5. **a)** Imagine you and your guide have just come upon a family of mountain gorillas. Brainstorm with a partner and list six adjectives that describe your feelings. Then list six verbs that describe what you will do in the next sixty seconds.

   b) Using the word lists you made in a), write a short paragraph about your meeting with the mountain gorillas.

Challenges with Words

1. Write the Super Words that match each clue. The shaded letters will spell a word that describes gorillas.

   a) a way of walking or running
   b) a large southern continent
   c) the opposite of freedom
   d) to find fault with
   e) the highest order of mammals
   f) wandered, roamed

2. Make four columns in your notebook like this.

one syllable	two syllables	three syllables	four syllables

Write each Super Word in the correct column. Mark the syllable we stress in each word.

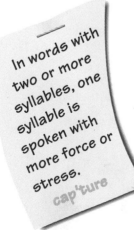

In words with two or more syllables, one syllable is spoken with more force or stress.

cap'ture

SUPER WORDS

Africa
captivity
complain
primates
gait
strayed

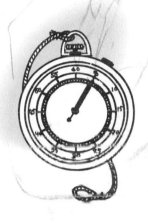

3. Many homophones have the spelling pattern **ai** or **a_e**.

Example: *The gorilla, with its shuffling **gait**, went through the **gate** of its cage.*

Gait and **gate** sound the same but have different spellings. When we write a homophone we must think about its meaning as well as its sound to spell the correct word.

Rewrite the paragraph below, using the correct homophones.

The unfriendly dog was not wagging its <u>tale</u> when I delivered <u>male</u> to the house. As the dog leaped at me I turned <u>pail</u>, and <u>maid</u> a flying leap through the gate—just like a <u>plain</u> taking off!

4. One–Two–Three–GO! Find as many words as you can with the **ay** pattern as in **stayed**. Give yourself five minutes.

5. The Super Word **primates** comes from the word **prime**, which means 'first in rank or order'. Find three words in the dictionary that have the base word **prime**. Write your own definitions for these words.

6. Finish this story with Super Words and your own words.

Far away, in the continent of _____ , there lived a small band of _____ . One day a young male _____ from the band and was captured and kept in _____ . The poor animal.....

7. These new words are all created by combining two simple words. Write the words that fit the sentences below.
   a) When you travel some airlines give you _____ _____ toward a free flight.
   b) _____ _____ may save lives in a car crash.
   c) Listening to a _____ _____ helps pass the time on a long car trip.

2

Long and Short e

e ee ea

lens   speed   heat

laser
sending
melt
metal
electric
speed
seemed
feeling
beam
seat
heat
disease
cheap
medical
lens
temperature

Exploring the Wonderful World of Lasers

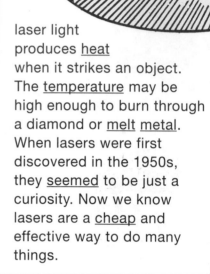

Imagine a <u>beam</u> of light that can burn a wart off your toe or change the shape of the <u>lens</u> in your eye—without your <u>feeling</u> a thing! A <u>laser</u> can perform these <u>medical</u> miracles. Besides their use in the fight against <u>disease</u>, lasers are used for many purposes. They can be used for <u>sending</u> high <u>speed</u> signals to the stars or for cutting out the cloth for the <u>seat</u> you are sitting on. Lasers are produced by <u>electric</u> current. The narrow laser light produces <u>heat</u> when it strikes an object. The <u>temperature</u> may be high enough to burn through a diamond or <u>melt</u> <u>metal</u>. When lasers were first discovered in the 1950s, they <u>seemed</u> to be just a curiosity. Now we know lasers are a <u>cheap</u> and effective way to do many things.

Observing Patterns

1. Write the list words that have three syllables. Which list word has four syllables?

2. Three list words have the sound /z/ spelled with the letter **s** as in **wise**. Write them.

3. Write the base word of each of the list words below.

sending   feeling   seemed

4. Write the list words that fit these definitions.
   a) an illness
   b) a very narrow and powerful beam of light
   c) the part of the eye, or a piece of glass, that controls the direction of light passing through it

Can you think of other words that fit each set?

5. Write a list word that goes with each set.

a) gold   copper   tin   _____

b) boiling   lukewarm   freezing   _____

c) camera   glasses   microscope   _____

6. Sometimes it is difficult to hear the vowel sounds in words. Complete each list word with the correct vowel and write the words in your notebook.

met _ l   **temp _ rat _ re**   **med _ c _ l**   **d _ sease**

7. Write the list words that fit these boxes.

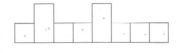

Discovering Patterns

laser sending melt metal electric
speed seemed feeling beam seat heat
disease cheap medical lens temperature

1. Write the list words that have the short vowel sound /e/ as in **lens**. Circle the letter that makes this sound.

2. Many of the list words have the long vowel sound /ē/ as in **seat**. The /ē/ sound can be spelled in more than one way. Write the /ē/ list words under two headings.

/ē/ spelled **ea** as in **meat**	/ē/ spelled **ee** as in **feet**

POWERBOOSTER

- The short vowel sound /e/ is usually spelled **e** as in **lens**.
- The long vowel sound /ē/ may be spelled **ea** as in **meat** or **ee** as in **feet**.

Exploring Patterns

1. Transform the word **seat** into **read** using seven steps. For each step change only one letter at a time. Read these clues to help you.

s e a t

a) drums and hearts do this _____ 　　 _ _ _ _

b) a laser _____ 　　 _ _ _ _

c) people working as a unit _____ 　　 _ _ _ _

d) saltwater drop from the eye _____ 　　 _ _ _ _

e) the feeling of being afraid _____ 　　 _ _ _ _

f) opposite of front _____ 　　 _ _ _ _

r e a d

2. Do you feel hungry? Here are some things for you to eat! Write the name of each **ee** or **ea** word in the picture.

3. The words below have the same bases as the list words **electric**, **metal**, and **medical**. Complete each sentence with one of the words. Write the sentence.

electricity	medicine
electrician	metallic

a) Don't forget to take your _____ at bedtime.

b) Our cabin in the woods has no _____.

c) The spaceship had a strange _____ glow.

d) We called an _____ to repair the stove.

4. Make a word pole with the word **temperature**. Add one weather word for each letter. The pole has been started for you.

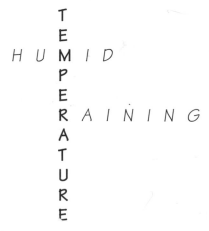

```
        T
        E
  H U M I D
        P
        E
        R A I N I N G
        A
        T
        U
        R
        E
```

Make up a personal list of interesting weather words.

8

SUPER WORDS

squeeze
treatment
energy
spectrum
feature
remote

5. Imagine you are in this spacecraft, orbiting Earth. You're having a problem with something on board and you want help from Earth. Write the message you might send to your control centre. Use some of these list words in your message.

temperature   electric   melt   metal   heat   sending

Challenges with Words

1. Write the Super Words that fit the sentences.

a) Lasers are high _____ light sources.

b) Someday, lasers might be used to send messages to _____ space stations.

c) A laser beam can be so narrow it can _____ through a tiny opening.

d) Laser equipment is used in the _____ of many diseases.

e) One _____ of the laser is the way it can burn through any material.

2. a) Write the Super Words that are synonyms for these words.

distant   pinch   remedy   power   highlight

b) Use each word or its synonym in a sentence of your own.

3. The letters in **laser** stand for **l**ight **a**mplification by **s**timulated **e**mission of **r**adiation. Words like this are called 'acronyms'.

Make up a definition for a word you use every day. Have the first letters in each word of your definition spell the word.

*Example: BIKE—**B**asic **I**ndividual **K**id's **E**njoyment*

9

4. Write a word with the long vowel sound /ē/ that fits these patterns.

　　a) It was (ee) cold as the wind howled through the (ee) in the forest.
　　b) Don't (ea) your little brother alone!
　　c) The goalie dropped to her (ee).
　　d) For years, the ship had sailed the high (ea).

5. Use the Super Words and your own words to finish this story.

The young scientist was proud of his invention. It was a water _____ method that would provide clean water for the city and conserve _____ at the same time. No longer would water be piped from a _____ lake high in the mountains. Water from deep wells would be used for most of the city's needs. Another special _____ of his invention was....

3 Long and Short i
i_e i
slide   cliff

fixed
practice
accident
grip
difficult
skill
fifth
cliff
equipment
quit
quickly
slide
line
guide
organized
spike

Exploring the Highest Mountain on Earth

What do you need to climb the highest mountain on Earth? Lots of <u>practice</u> on less difficult mountains and good <u>equipment</u>! The first Canadian team to climb Mount Everest in 1982 had both of these. They were also well organized and refused to <u>quit</u>, even when an <u>accident</u> claimed the lives of four team members. The Canadian team needed all of their <u>skill</u> to climb the Khumbu icefall. To get a <u>grip</u> on a <u>cliff</u> of ice they often had to drive a <u>spike</u> into the ice and attach a safety <u>line</u>. With this <u>fixed</u> rope to <u>guide</u> them, the team members could move more <u>quickly</u> up the mountain. The climb was divided into five stages. The <u>fifth</u> stage was the final climb to the summit. Near the peak, they faced the danger of a <u>slide</u> from the narrow ridge. Finally, on October 5, 1982, Laurie Skreslet, Sungdare, and Lhakpa Dorje, stood on the highest spot in the world.

Observing Patterns

1. Write the seven list words that would appear in the dictionary after the word **mountain**.

2. Write the four list words that have three syllables.

3. Ski down the mountain! At every turn, fill in the missing letters of a list word.

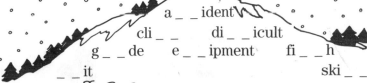

a _ _ ident
cli _ _   di _ _ icult
g _ _ de   e _ _ ipment   fi _ _ h
_ _ it   ski _ _

4. Write the list words that complete the story and fit the shapes.

We had a final [_____] before going over the

edge of the [_____] . I [_____] the ropes

firmly around a rock, checked my safety

[_____] , and tied the safety

[_____] to my harness. Then I checked my [____]

and started to slide [_____] down the slope.

Discovering Patterns

*fixed practice accident grip difficult
skill fifth cliff equipment quit
quickly slide line guide organized spike*

1. Write the list words that have the short vowel sound /i/ as in **trick**. Circle the letter that makes this sound.

2. Write the five list words that have the long vowel sound /ī/ as in **kite**. What letters spell the /ī/ sound in these words?

3. Write the list words that have the sound /kw/ as in **quick**. Underline the letters that make this sound.

How many words can you write that start with qu?

POWERBOOSTER

- The sound /i/ is usually spelled **i** as in **trick**.
- The sound /ī/ may be spelled **i_e** as in **kite**.
- The sound /kw/ is spelled **qu** as in **quick**.

Exploring Patterns

1. Complete this limerick. The first two words are list words.
There was a young boy from Kilbride.
Who loved to climb up the big _____ .
And there he would sit
Not wanting to _____ ,
Yet wishing for somewhere to _____ .

2. Can you meet this challenge? Draw the chart in your notebook, then complete the chart with the base form of the verbs and their past tense forms.

Base Word	Past Tense Form
fix	_____
_____	gripped
guide	_____
_____	slid
_____	organized

3. Climb this ladder. For each rung write a word that has the sound /kw/ spelled **qu**. Check the spelling of the new words in a dictionary.

a) the sound made by a duck

b) neither a solid nor a gas

c) neither more nor less

d) rectangle with equal sides

e) opposite of answer

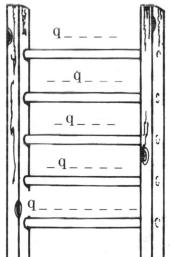

q _ _ _ _

_ _ q _ _ _

_ q _ _ _

_ q _ _ _ _

q _ _ _ _ _ _

4. Write the list words that complete each analogy.
a) **second** is to **third** as **fourth** is to _____
b) **injured** is to **healed** as **broken** is to _____
c) **quietly** is to **loudly** as **slowly** is to _____

_____
Fingers are
to hands as
toes are to
feet is an
example of an
analogy.

5. What thoughts are going through the mind of this mountaineer? Write a few sentences that put her thoughts into words. Use some of the list words below.

difficult   quickly   grip   cliff   slide

6. a) Many things you do require skill, practice, and good equipment, just as mountaineering does. Choose a physical activity you like and list in a chart the things you need to do it well. When you are finished you will have notes about your favourite activity.

Example: **soccer**

Skills	Practice	Equipment
kicking, running	every day	soccer ball, shoes

b) Now write a paragraph about your favourite activity.

Challenges with Words

1. Use the Super Words to complete the story. Then match the letters in each word to the numbered spaces below to name the two men who first climbed Mount Everest.

The Conquerors of Everest

Mount Everest has a _ 1 _ _ _ _ 8 _ rise of 8848 metres. Many mountain _ 7 _ 3 _ _ _ _ have tried to reach its summit. The first _ _ _ 12 10 for the top was in 1922, but that _ _ _ _ 2 _ _ _ 11 _ was unsuccessful. It wasn't until 1953 that two men, neither of them a _ 4 _ _ _ _ _ 9, finally conquered the mountain. Imagine the _ _ _ 6 _ _ _ _ 5 _ of being the first to reach the top!

_ _ _   _ _ _ _ _ _   H _ _ _ _ _ Y
12 6 9   1 2 3 4 5 2   6 7 7 8 9

_ _ _ Z   _ _ G   _ _ _ G _ Y
10 1 5   6 5   5 11 9   8

quest
quitter
excitement
expedition
climbers
vertical

2. Write synonyms for these 'mountain' words.

hazardous   difficult   highest   immense

Create your own list of four 'mountain' words and their synonyms.

3. Sometimes we add **-er** when we want to describe someone who does something. Sometimes we add **-or**. Write as many of these words you can think of in ten minutes. *Example: Climbers are people who climb.*
but
Actors are people who act.

-or	-er
editor	winner

4. a) The word **excite** is blowing its top like a volcano! Write 'exciting' words by adding the endings or suffixes at the base of the volcano.

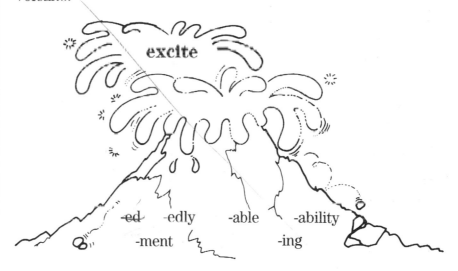

excite

-ed   -edly   -able   -ability
-ment   -ing

b) Use some of these 'exciting' words in a paragraph about a thrilling adventure or quest, perhaps to the top of a mountain.

5. The new words all contain long vowels. Write the words that fit the clues.
  a) I have a long **a** and a long **i**.
  b) I have a long **o** and a long **a**.
  c) I have a long **a**.

NEW WORDS

trail bike
skateboard
rollerblading

4

Long o
o_e   oa
smoke   coal

modern
solid
deposits
promise
copper
wrote
bulldozer
smoke
whole
explodes
loaded
coal
Mexico
machine
locate
goal

Exploring the World of Prospecting

The <u>modern</u> gold hunter is looking for veins, or 'showings', of silver, <u>copper</u>, and other minerals. Prospectors know that these veins are like a message that nature <u>wrote</u> millions of years ago—"Look for gold here." They know that when they <u>locate</u> one precious mineral, there is a <u>promise</u> of a <u>whole</u> range of other minerals close by. Gold <u>deposits</u> are often deep in <u>solid</u> rock. These hard rock mines are safe compared to <u>coal</u> mines, or other mines in loose, softer rock. But the gold is hard to obtain. Miners have to drill deep holes in the rock, and pack them with dynamite. When the dynamite <u>explodes</u>, part of the tunnel is blown away. After the <u>smoke</u> clears, the gold ore is scooped up by a <u>machine</u> like a small <u>bulldozer</u>, <u>loaded</u> into ore cars, and taken to the surface. The first gold in the western hemisphere was found in South and Central American countries such as <u>Mexico</u>. Since 1900, many gold mines have been discovered in northern Canada.

Observing Patterns

1. Write the eight list words that have two syllables. Put a mark over the syllable that is stressed.

Example: pícture begín

2. Use the clues on the gold nuggets to find list words.

/r/ spelled **wr** as in **wrist**   /h/ spelled **wh** as in **who**   /sh/ spelled **ch** as in **chute**

3. Answer this riddle with a list word: What do you call a calf's father who is sleeping?

4. Write the list words that fit these shapes.

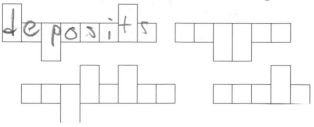

deposits

5. Build words on the word **explodes**. Use as many list words as you can. One example is done for you.

```
        E
        X
        P
        L
        O
        D
    M O D E R N
        E
        S
```

Discovering Patterns

modern solid deposits promise copper wrote bulldozer smoke whole explodes loaded coal Mexico machine locate goal

1. Write the list words that have the short vowel sound /o/ as in **stock**. Circle the letter that makes this sound.

2. Make a chart like the one below. Write the list words that have the long vowel sound /ō/ as in **hope** under the right headings.

/ō/ spelled **o_e** as in **hole**	/ō/ spelled **oa** as in **boat**	/ō/ spelled **o** as in **piano**

POWERBOOSTER

- The short vowel sound /o/ is usually spelled **o** as in **stock**.
- The long vowel sound /ō/ may be spelled **o_e** as in **hope**, **oa** as in **boat**, or **o** as in **piano**.

17

Exploring Patterns

1. Combine the letters on the pennies with the long /ō/ patterns on the gold coins to make words with the long **o** sound.

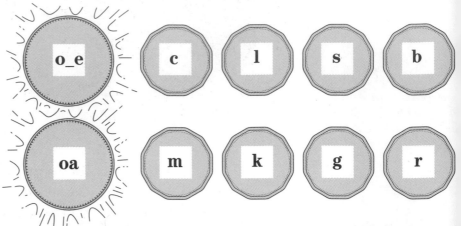

2. A word web contains words and phrases that go with the word at the centre. Make a word web for these list words: **bulldozer moder**

Example:

saves work   repairs

machine ⟶ industry

car   motor

3. Many words can be 'exploded' to form new words. These words are all related to the list word **locate**.

Complete each sentence below with the correct word. You will find this word by adding suffixes or prefixes to the base word **locate**.

a) We decided this was the perfect _____ to look for gold.
b) The _____ people told us there was no gold in the area.
c) We then decided to _____ our base in another area.
d) While I was digging for gold I _____ my back.

4. Sometimes the meaning of a word suggests a shape. Write these list words in shapes that suggest their meaning.

smoke   **explode**

Example:

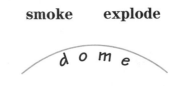

underground
explosion
prospector
propose
loaves
discovery

5. This prospector is in for a surprise. The fire that he lit last night is melting down through the snow to solid rock. When he scrapes back the ashes in the morning to make a new fire, he'll see something gleaming through the black soot. Gold! Write the message this prospector might send back to his family or friends.

Challenges with Words

1. Looking for gold, or what? Use the clues below to help you find your way through the shafts to the mother lode.

1. a large blast
2. subterranean
3. someone who looks for precious metals
4. suggest
5. large masses of bread
6. something discovered

2. Some words that end in **f** make their plurals by changing the **f** to **v** and adding -**es**. Write plurals that end in **ves** to fit the sentences below.

    a) Armand cut the pie into two _____ .   h _ _ _ _ _

    b) The gang of _____ robbed the bank.   t _ _ _ _ _ _

    c) One of the bookcase _____ was empty.   s _ _ _ _ _ _

    d) The whole wheat _____ were half price.   l _ _ _ _ _

    e) Handle the sharp _____ with care.   k _ _ _ _ _

3. Write sentences of your own with the plural forms of these words.

self wolf leaf life calf

4. Add prefixes and suffixes to the word **cover** to make as many words as you can. How many did you discover?

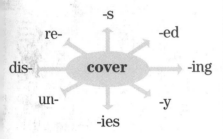

━━━━━━━━━━◀**WORDS IN HISTORY**━━━━━━

Discovery is made from the base word **cover**. According to the general rule, the **v** should be doubled to keep the sound of the **o** short. In Old English the doubled **v** looked the same as a **w**. To keep the word from looking like **cower**, the **v** was kept single.

5. You found this map in the burned-out remains of Jim's cabin. Use the Super Words and your own words to tell how you discovered the Crazy Moose Mine.

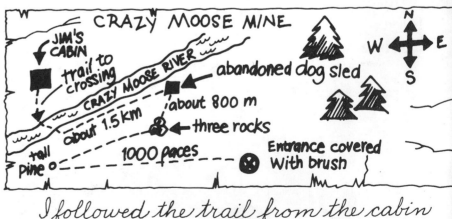

I followed the trail from the cabin door to the Crazy Moose River. There I...

5

Long u
u_e   ew   ue
include   crew   blue

dumb

skull

luck

huge

include

rules

continue

reduce

knew

crew

drew

glue

argue

thumb

jewels

blue

Exploring the Exciting World of the Pirates

Sailors in the <u>blue</u> waters of the Caribbean Sea and the Gulf of Mexico <u>knew</u> the dreaded sign of the <u>skull</u> and crossbones on a pirate flag. When they met a pirate ship, the <u>crew</u> could only watch as a fierce gang of buccaneers came aboard, <u>drew</u> their swords, and carried off <u>huge</u> treasures of gold and <u>jewels</u>. If they tried to <u>argue</u>, they might find themselves walking the plank! Pirates stuck together like <u>glue</u> and there were strict <u>rules</u> that all pirates followed. For example, when they divided up the stolen goods, the pirates who had lost an eye, or even a <u>thumb</u> in battle, received a larger share. With <u>luck</u>, pirates could <u>continue</u> their adventurous lives until they were rich, but most came to a bad end. Famous pirates <u>include</u> Blackbeard, Captain Kidd, Mary Read, and Anne Booney. Kidd may have hidden his treasure on Oak Island off Nova Scotia's coast, but no one has been able to find it.

Observing Patterns

1. Homophones are words that sound the same but are spelled differently and have different meanings. Write the list words that are homophones for the words **new** and **blew**.

2. Write the two list words that have the sound /m/ spelled **mb**.

3. Write the list words that have two or more syllables. Put a mark over the syllable that is stressed.

Example: *mágic repéat*

4. Complete these sets with list words. Write the list word that goes with the words in each treasure chest.

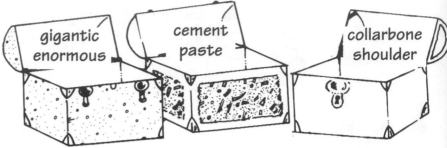

gigantic
enormous

cement
paste

collarbone
shoulder

Discovering Patterns

dumb skull luck huge include
rules continue reduce knew crew
drew glue argue thumb jewels blue

1. Write the four list words that have the short vowel sound /u/ as in **truck**. Circle the letter that makes this sound.

2. Make two charts like the ones below in your notebook. Add to your first chart the list words that have the long vowel sound /ü/ as in **spoon**. Add to your second chart the list words that have the sound /yü/ as in **huge**.

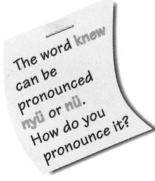

The word knew can be pronounced nyü or nü. How do you pronounce it?

/ü/ spelled **u_e** as in **salute**	/ü/ spelled **ew** as in **flew**	/ü/ spelled **ue** as in **true**

/yü/ spelled **u_e** as in **mule**	/yü/ spelled **ew** as in **few**	/yü/ spelled **ue** as in **cue**

POWERBOOSTER

- The short vowel sound /u/ is usually spelled **u** as in **truck**.
- The long vowel sound /ü/ may be spelled **u_e** as in **rule**, **ew** as in **flew**, or **ue** as in **blue**.
- The long vowel sound /yü/ may be spelled **u_e** as in **mule**, **ew** as in **few**, or **ue** as in **cue**.

Exploring Patterns

1. Write the word in each set which has the sound /ü/ as in **crew**, **glue**, and **rule** or /yü/ as in **mule**, **few**, and **cue**. Circle the first letter of each answer. Then copy down the circled letters to find the answer to this question.

What was the sound that Captain Hook feared the most in the story *Peter Pan*?   _ _ _k _ _ _k

a) crust	true	shoulder
b) trouble	clumsy	include
c) clue	outside	rumble
d) would	rusty	threw
e) overdue	shook	buckle
f) should	cute	doubt

2. Complete this pirate story with list words. Write the story in your notebook.

The captain _____ an X over a tree on the treasure map. He and his _____ of pirates _____ they would find a chest of precious _____ buried near that tree. With any _____ , they would soon be rich! They found the tree and dug up a box. But instead of _____ , they found only a note with a drawing of a human _____ on it. The note was written in code.

3. Decode the message in the treasure chest using the code below.

27	26	25	24	23	22	21	20	19	18	17	16	15
A	B	C	D	E	F	G	H	I	J	K	L	M

14	13	12	11	10	9	8	7	6	5	4	3	2	1
N	O	P	Q	R	S	T	U	V	W	X	Y	Z	!

```
3  13  7       16  19  23      27  14  24       3  13  7
__ __ __       __  __  __      __  __  __       __ __ __

25  20  23  27  8       27  14  24      26  10  23  27  17      27  16  16
__  __  __  __  __      __  __  __      __  __  __  __  __      __  __  __

8  20  23      10  7  16  23  9      14  13  5
__ __ __       __  __ __  __  __     __  __ __

9  13  15  23  26  13  24  3      23  16  9  23      20  27  9
__ __  __  __  __  __  __  __     __  __  __ __     __  __ __

8  27  17  23  14       8  20  23      18  23  5  23  16  9  1
__ __  __  __  __       __  __  __     __  __  __  __  __  __ __
```

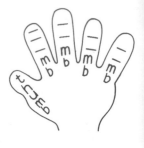

4. In **thumb** and **dumb** the sound /m/ is spelled **mb**. Write a word for each clue below that ends in **mb**.

- object used to tidy your hair
- part of a tree
- baby sheep
- to go up, using hands and feet.

5. a) Beginning with the buckle on the pirate's boots, or the plume on the hat, describe a swashbuckling pirate captain from toe to head or from head to toe.

When you write a description of how someone looks, be sure to use lots of colour, size, and shape words, so that the reader can picture the person. It will also help your reader if you keep your description in order. For example: head, body, legs, feet.

b) You may wish to draw the pirate captain after you have written your description.

Challenges with Words

1. Write the Super Words that fit the blanks in the sentences.

a) With the crash of _____ , the storm caught us unaware.

b) All the pirate's _____ needed was a black eye patch.

c) A _____ in gold and silver was buried on the island.

d) We had a _____ of the entire island from the hilltop.

e) The shipment of gold was _____ in England in October.

f) After three months at sea, our _____ were almost gone.

2. Fortune Hunt! For each letter of the Super Word **fortune**, write a word or phrase for things that you might find in a pirate's treasure chest.

f _____

o _____

r _____

t _____

u _____

n _____

e _____

due
costume
view
supplies
thunder ✓
fortune

3. Make a list of words that are connected to pirates. Use them to make a crossword puzzle. Test it and make an answer key.

Example:

¹a		³s		
²f	l	a	g	
t		i		
		l		

Across
2. A Jolly Roger is one.

Down
1. Toward the back of a ship.
3. Wind fills a _____ .

4. Do you know these homophones? Several letter combinations make the sound /ü/ or /yü/. Write the words that fit the blanks.
   a) Sparks _____ in all directions.
   b) The morning _____ made everything damp.
   c) The sky at sunset has a rosy _____.
   d) Our history project on pirates is _____ tomorrow.
   e) Smoke curled up the chimney _____ .
   f) The pioneers had to _____ wood with an axe.

hue
dew
flue
hew
due
flow

5. A ship's log is a record of what happens aboard ship. Below is the log from the pirate ship *Aztec Raider* carrying gold and silver from Mexico. Complete the log, using as many Super Words as you can.

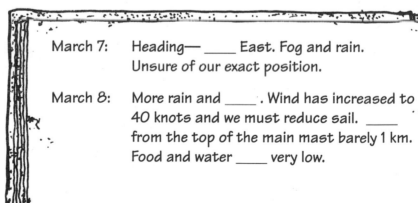

March 7:   Heading— ____ East. Fog and rain. Unsure of our exact position.

March 8:   More rain and ____ . Wind has increased to 40 knots and we must reduce sail. ____ from the top of the main mast barely 1 km. Food and water ____ very low.

ozone layer

music video

microchip

6. All of the new words contain long vowel sounds. Write the words that fit the clues. Circle the long vowels.
   a) has the long **i** and long **o** sound.
   b) has the long **u** and long **o** sound.
   c) has the long **o** and long **a** sound.

Here is a list of words that may have been hard for you in Units 1–5. You and your teacher may add other words to the list.

accident	difficult	temperature	thumb
equipment	disease	guide	knew
gorilla	electric	whole	wrote
capture	fifth	jewels	argue

1. Use the Study Steps for each word. Your teacher will dictate the words.

2. Complete each sentence with words from the Study List that match the shape and suit the meaning. Write the sentences in your notebook.

a) The doctor ⬚⬚⬚ the boy's illness would be ⬚⬚⬚⬚⬚ to treat. The boy had a high ⬚⬚⬚⬚⬚⬚ and his ⬚⬚⬚ body shook with chills.

b) "You can avoid having an ⬚⬚⬚⬚⬚⬚ at work by using proper ⬚⬚⬚⬚⬚⬚," ⬚⬚⬚ the manager.

c) The zookeeper wanted to ⬚⬚⬚ the ⬚⬚⬚ to treat its sore ⬚⬚⬚.

3. Write the study words that have three or more syllables. Put a mark over the syllable that is stressed.

Example: con´tinue

4. a) Make a chart like this in your notebook.

/ā/ spelled as in **base, stay,** or **fail**	/ē/ spelled as in **beam** or **speed**	/ō/ spelled as in **smoke, coat,** or **Mexico**

b) Put the words below into the correct column on your chart.

bulldozer	display	piano	seemed
remain	goalie	disease	explode
dream	feeling	basement	trailer

5. Use each clue to find a letter. Then use the letters and the code to find the answer to the riddle below.

This letter is in **goal** but not in **log.** 1 _

This letter is in **dumb** but not in **drum.** 2 _

This letter is in **line** but not in **file.** 3 _

This letter is in **whole** but not in **lower.** 4 _

This letter is in **glue** but not in **leg.** 5 _

This letter is in **metal** but not in **trailer.** 6 _

This letter is in **quit** but not in **quickly.** 7 _

Question: What do you get when there's a hole in your mitten?

Answers: _   _   _   _   _   _   _   _   _   _

      1   3   5   6   2   7   4   5   6   2

6. Each picture word contains the sound /ü/ as in **blue** and **drew,** or /yü/ as in **huge** and **few.** Write the words.

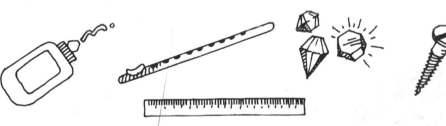

7. Write the word in each set that has the sound /ī/ as in **spike.**

a) linen   line   skinny

b) quit   quickly   guide

c) slide   slippery   slither

Dictionary Skills

1. Alphabetical Order: Write the review words from the Study List that would be found in the dictionary between each set of words below.

apple / coal	deposits / every
furnace / hair	task / write

2. Guide Words: Every page in a dictionary has a set of guide words at the top of it. The guide word **captive** on the left is the first entry on that page. The guide word **cave** on the right is the last entry on the page.

For each picture in the left column, write the correct set of guide words.

a) janitor / jacket;   jeans / jigsaw; joker / junk

b) slide / solid;   seemed / skill; sending / smoke

c) violin / volcano;   vacuum / vampire; vanish / victim

3. Word Meaning: A dictionary gives the meanings or definitions of the entry words. Most entry words have more than one meaning. The different meanings for an entry word help us to understand the word better and tell us how it can be used in different ways.

Read the entry for the word **beam**.

> **beam** (bēm)   **1** a radio signal used to guide aircraft, ships, etc. **2** a ray of light or heat **3** look or smile brightly **4** the main horizontal support of a building or ship

Write the definition of **beam** used in each of these sentences.

a) The child's face beamed with delight.
b) Laser beams are used to treat some diseases.
c) They walked along the beams in the attic.
d) The captain used the beams to change course.

Exploring the World of Inventions

1. Brainstorm with your group to list as many important recent inventions as you can. Sort your inventions into categories. For example:

Communications	Electronics	Medicine
the Internet	CD player	ultrasound

2. Imagine you have perfected an amazing new invention which will change the world. Write a description of your invention. Describe it from top to bottom or left to right. You will probably want to include a diagram of your invention.

3. Edit your description carefully to make sure your sentences are clear and interesting.

Grammar Power

1. Writing with common and proper nouns: We use a **noun** to name a **person**, **place**, or **thing**.

A **common noun** names a person, place, or thing. A **proper noun** is a special name, place, or thing.

	Common Nouns	Proper Nouns
Person	man	Bruno
Place	country	Mexico
Thing	magazine	National Geographic

Make two columns in your notebook and sort the nouns below into the correct column.

Common Nouns	Proper Nouns

John	Alberta	sister	hospital
gorilla	thumb	Simi	Stanley Cup
island	Vancouver	Uncle Elvis	Glenbow Museum

2. Complete these sentences by adding either a common or a proper noun. These nouns will be the **subject** of the sentence, or what the sentence is about.

　　a) _____ jumped over the fence.

　　b) _____ zoomed down the highway.

　　c) _____ ate fried worms.

　　d) _____ wore a ridiculous hat.

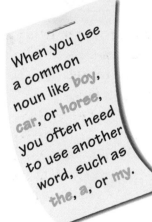

When you use a common noun like boy, car, or horse, you often need to use another word, such as the, a, or my.

3. Using Abstract Nouns: Some nouns name things such as courage, or happiness, that we can't touch, smell, see, hear, or taste. These are called abstract nouns. In Units 1 – 6 you studied the following abstract nouns:

luck   promise   skill   practice

Unscramble the words in the sentences below.

    a) This computer game requires **lslik** and **clku** to win!

    b) I **miserop** you will have time to attend the next **rcatcpie**.

4. Write your own definition for the abstract noun **happiness**. Here are some sample definitions.

Happiness is a warm puppy. (Charlie Brown)

Happiness is getting everything you want for your birthday.

Happiness is _____. (your own definition)

Proofing Power

The following paragraph was written by a student in Grade 4. Read it carefully, rewriting words that are spelled incorrectly. Compare your list of misspellings with a partner.

> Yesterday my mother and I went to a museum. It was dificult to find. i new we were going the wrong way, but I didnt want to argew. When we got there, a giude helpt us find the displays. I think the best exhibit was about inventions. It had lots of expensive eqippment and I new it must have cost a hole lot of money. We decideed to go to the animel exhibit next. There was a statue of a gorila. When I askt why they didn't have a real one, the man said they were very rare and dificult to capchur. At the end the gide handed us a form that asked, "Did you have a good time today at the museum?" I rote, "Yes!"

7 Vowels with r
ar ir ur er ear

art **cir**cle **sur**face
larg**er** s**ear**ch

apart
against
larger
certain
perhaps
eastern
dirt
circle
surface
search
earliest
remarkable
earth
desert
surprise
often

Exploring the Fossil Record of Early Human Beings

In Africa, scientists have discovered skeletons of perhaps the earliest human beings on Earth. No one is certain, but it seems these remarkable fossil bones found on the eastern plains of Africa are more than a million years old. This is a surprise. Until recently, many scientists believed that human history only went back about 10 000 years. Sometimes these bones are found near the surface of the ground, sometimes deep in caves. Although a few larger pieces, such as lower jawbones, are uncovered intact, usually the skeletons have been broken into tiny pieces and these are found far apart. Workers must search through layers of dirt and desert sand in an ever-widening circle to recover each piece, then fit them together like a jigsaw puzzle. Often, they must race against time to save valuable fossil records from bulldozers and building crews.

Observing Patterns

1. Write the five list words that have the stress on the second syllable. Place a stress mark over the second syllable.

2. Write the list words that begin with the sound /s/. Circle the letter that makes the /s/ sound in each word.

3. Write the list word that means the opposite of the underlined word or phrase in each sentence.
   a) Their <u>latest</u> discovery was quite remarkable.
   b) Some people think that the mythical lost city of Atlantis lies on the <u>floor</u> of the ocean.
   c) We are <u>not sure</u> what caused the destruction of the Inca civilization.

Think of your own words to add to each set.

4. Write the list word that belongs in each set.
   a) taller heavier younger _____
   b) sand cactus heat _____
   c) triangle oval square _____
   d) mud sand clay _____
   e) always regularly frequently _____

5. Complete each list word below.

de _ ert   s _ _ pri _ e   ag _ _ nst   _ ert _ _ n   o _ _ en

Discovering Patterns

apart against larger certain perhaps eastern dirt circle surface search earliest remarkable earth desert surprise often

1. Write the list words that have the sound /är/ as in **farm**. Circle the letters that make this sound.

2. Many of the list words have the sound /èr/ as in **bird**. The /èr/ sound can be spelled in more than one way. Write the /èr/ list words in under the following headings.

/èr/ spelled er as in **term**	/èr/ spelled ir as in **bird**	/èr/ spelled ur as in **burn**	/èr/ spelled ear as in **earth**

POWERBOOSTER

- The sound /är/ is usually spelled **ar** as in **chart**.
- The sound /èr/ may be spelled **er** as in **term**, **ir** as in **bird**, **ur** as in **burn**, or **ear** as in **earth**.

Exploring Patterns

1. Solve this puzzle with /ėr/ words spelled **ir**, **ur**, **er**, or **ear**.
   a) the day you were born _ _ _ _ _ _ _ _
   b) the name of our planet _ _ _ _ _
   c) how you feel when you are worried or afraid _ _ _ _ _ _ _
   d) a colour made by mixing red and blue _ _ _ _ _ _
   e) tables, chairs, beds, etc. _ _ _ _ _ _ _ _ _

2. The suffixes -**er** and -**est** can be added to base words to mean **more** and **most**.

   Example: early, earlier, earliest
   large, larger, largest

   Notice that words which end in **y** change the **y** to **i** when adding -**er** and -**est**. Words which end in **e** drop the **e** before adding -**er** and -**est**. Complete the sets with -**er** and -**est** words.

   dark _____ _____
   dirty _____ _____
   smart _____ _____
   late _____ _____

3. The list word **circle** comes from the Latin word <u>circus</u>. Draw a circus picture to show how <u>circus</u> and **circle** are connected in meaning.

4. The suffix -**able** is added to many words to make them mean 'can be' or 'able to'.

   Add -**able** to the words below and use them in the proper sentences. Write the sentences in your notebook.

return	wash
remark	love

   a) I'm glad my new sweater is made of _____ material.
   b) The anthropologist made a _____ discovery that changed the way we think about early humans.
   c) Are these pop bottles _____ or should we recycle them?
   d) My new puppy is so cuddly and _____ .

Remember: Earth with a capital E is the planet and earth with a lower case e is soil.

Remember to drop the e when adding -able to love — lovable.

5. Imagine you are whisked backward to the time of cave dwellers. You find yourself in a smoky cave, and see some figures sitting around a fire. Right behind you is your time machine. You have a choice. You can return to your own time immediately, or do some exploring of the cave dwellers' world. Write a few sentences explaining the choice you would make and your reasons for it. Use some of these list words in your sentences.

circle   **earliest**   **surprise**   **perhaps**   **against**

Challenges with Words

1. Match the Super Words to the sentences below.

a) The _____ water of the rapids made it difficult to cross the river.

b) The workers _____ the hole until the entire skeleton was uncovered.

c) _____ is an important element found in all living matter and can sometimes be used to tell the age of a fossil.

d) During the last ice age, few species _____ the cold in the north.

e) Scientists spend much time doing _____ on early humans.

f) The backbone is made up of many _____ .

2. Mark the stressed vowel in each Super Word you wrote for exercise 1. Compare your list with a partner's. If you don't agree about the stress of any word, check the dictionary. Which Super Word can have the stress on either syllable?

Proofread your sentences with a partner.

carbon
enlarged
research
swirling
vertebrae
survived

3. Plurals are interesting. **Vertebrae** is the plural of **vertebra**, a word we seldom use in its singular form. Write the words below. Circle the one you think is the plural form in each pair. Then check it in your dictionary.

bacteria, bacterium   data, datum   alga, algae
fungus, fungi   hippopotamus, hippopotami

4. Brainstorm with a partner to think of twenty words that have to do with searching for fossil bones. Then make a word search for another set of partners to solve. Give them a time limit to find all the words.

f			
o			
s	a	n	d
s			i
i			g
l			

5. **Research** is an investigation of a subject. Using classroom or library reference materials, research these topics.

Subject: Animal classification
Find two animals for each of the following categories:

- mammals
- reptiles
- amphibians
- birds
- insects

6. New words from the computer world are added to our language all the time. Match the new words to their original meaning. Then write a brief definition of each word as you use it to refer to computers or people who use them.
a) the top of a desk
b) nuts, bolts, nails, etc.
c) a person who chops things in pieces

NEW WORDS

hardware

hacker

desktop

Vowels with r
or   ar   our
shore   darkness   four

Arctic
darkness
shore
force
order
before
explore
support
forever
north
warmest
four
aboard
outdoors
iceberg
quarter

Exploring the Arctic World

Inside the <u>Arctic</u> Circle the sun never rises on December 21st. There is <u>darkness</u> for twenty-four hours. Further <u>north</u>, toward the North Pole, this polar night may last a <u>quarter</u> of the year or longer. Instead of <u>four</u> seasons, in the Arctic world there are two—a winter that seems to last <u>forever</u> and a short, cool summer. But even though the summer is only two months long, the Arctic can <u>support</u> a wide variety of plant and animal life, such as wildflowers, foxes, lemmings, and caribou. The children who live along the <u>shore</u> of the Arctic Ocean enjoy being <u>outdoors</u> during this <u>warmest</u> part of the year. They can jump <u>aboard</u> boats to go fishing, watch an <u>iceberg</u> more than a kilometre long float by, or <u>explore</u> the tundra. They know that <u>before</u> long winter storms will sweep across the Arctic with terrible <u>force</u> as the sun sinks close to the horizon once more. Long winters followed by short summers—this <u>order</u>, or pattern, is something people in the Arctic know well.

Observing Patterns

1. Write the list words that have the sound /är/ as in **parka**.

2. Which list word was borrowed from the Dutch word <u>ijsberg</u> and means 'mountain of ice'?

3. Write the list words that would be found in the dictionary between the words below.

    express / freeze   nature / question

35

4. Complete the list words on each polar bear.

_ b _ _ rd
f _ _ r

su _ _ ort
q _ _ rter

Ar _ t _ _

Discovering Patterns

Arctic darkness shore force order before explore support forever north warmest four aboard outdoors iceberg quarter

1. Many of the list words have the sound /ôr/ as in **store**. Write the /ôr/ list words which fit under either of these headings.

/ôr/ spelled **ore** as in **store**	/ôr/ spelled **or** as in **horse**

2. There are a number of ways to spell the /ôr/ sound, such as **ar** and **our**. Words which use these other patterns are called **irregular** forms. Write the list words which spell the /ôr/ sound using **ar** and **our**. Underline the letters which make the /ôr/ sound in each word.

3. Look through the story again and find other words that have the /ôr/ sound. Underline the letters that spell this sound.

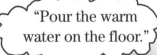

"Pour the warm water on the floor."

POWERBOOSTER

- The sound /ôr/ is usually spelled **ore** as in **store** or **or** as in **horse**.
- Irregular forms of the /ôr/ sound are **ar** as in **warn**, **our** as in **four**, **oar** as in **roar**, **oor** as in **floor**.

Exploring Patterns

1. It's just the tip of the iceberg! Combine the letters below the surface of the ocean with the /ôr/ patterns on the tip of the iceberg to create more words with the /ôr/ sound.

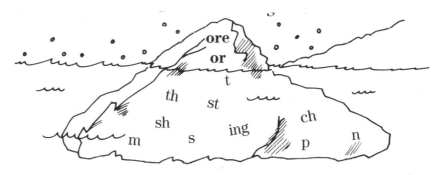

2. Write the list word that completes each analogy.
   a) **Four** is to **two** as **half** is to _____ .
   b) **Grass** is to **lawn** as **sand** is to _____ .
   c) **Light** is to **darkness** as **after** is to _____ .

3. The prefix **ex-** usually means 'out' or 'out of'. The list word **explore**, for example, means 'to search beyond'. Replace the underlined words or phrases in each sentence with a word from below. Write the sentences.

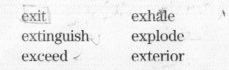

exit	exhale
extinguish	explode
exceed	exterior

   a) We plan to paint the <u>outside</u> of our house.
   b) Do you know where the <u>way out</u> is?
   c) The mass of your suitcase must not <u>go beyond</u> twenty kilograms.
   d) The firefighters worked quickly to <u>put out</u> the blaze.
   e) Take a deep breath, and then <u>let the air out</u>.
   f) If you throw that spray can in the fire, it could <u>blow apart</u>.

4. Make a word web for the list words **darkness**, **Arctic**, and **outdoors**. Sometimes you can make smaller webs with the words you add.

Example:

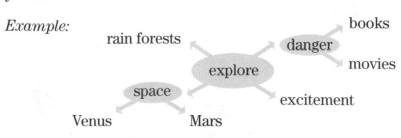

Think of other analogies with list words.

37

5. Suppose you have to spend six weeks of endless polar nights in a weather station near the North Pole. There is plenty of food and fuel in the hut, but nothing else. What supplies and equipment will you take to keep yourself from getting too bored? List everything you might want for entertainment indoors. Now imagine you have to carry it three kilometres from your landing strip. Whittle your list down to three or four things you could easily backpack.

Things I'd like to Take	Things I Could Carry

Challenges with Words

1. Match the Super Words to the word sets below. Then add one or two of your own words to each set.

a) land   space   _____

b) visible   exterior   _____

c) alien   unknown   _____

d) fear   terror   _____

e) Europe   Asia   _____

f) eastern   western   _____

2. Write the Super Word that has the letter **c** in two places.

Antarctica
horror
unexplored
territory
outward
northern

━━━━━ **WORDS IN HISTORY** ━━━━━

The word **Arctic** comes from the word <u>Arktos</u>, which was the ancient Greek word for 'bear', and the name for the constellation of the Guardian of the Bear in the northern skies. The prefix **anti-** means 'opposite', so **Antarctica** was the name given to the continent surrounding the South Pole.

3. The sound /ôr/ can be spelled in many ways. Find words that are **opposites** of the words below. Each one will contain the /ôr/ sound.

    a) excited or interested   b **ored**

    b) ceiling   f _____

    c) fall or descend   s _____

    d) the outside layer   c _____

    e) pay attention   i _____

    f) cool   w_____

4. For each letter of the word ANTARCTICA write the name of a country or continent.

A **frica** _____

N _____

T _____

A _____

R _____

C _____

T **rinidad** _____

I _____

C _____

A _____

5. What other words do you think of when you hear the Super Word **northern**. Write the words, then make a triangle poem by organizing some of your words into the shape of a triangle.

Example:

Northern

_____ _____

_____ _____ _____

_____ _____ _____ _____

6. Use the Super Words to finish this story about an expedition to reach the South Pole by crossing Antarctica.

All night the wind howled across the frozen wasteland of _____ . By morning, there was no sign of our tents and vehicles. We were lost in the vast _____ of this _____ continent. We only had enough supplies to....

9

Long and Short e
e_e ey y ea
supreme   journey   carry
ahead

ahead
already
death
wearing
instead
complete
supreme
athlete
journey
hockey
carry
everywhere
especially
finally
suddenly
body

The Vikings

Did you ever wonder why hockey and other sports teams are sometimes called 'the Vikings'? A Viking was the supreme athlete of a thousand years ago, strong and determined. Viking settlers had already reached the shores of northern Newfoundland by the year 1000. How did they make this incredible journey? Not in jets, or modern ships. Instead, they came in small longboats that could carry them everywhere. They sailed across oceans and rowed up shallow rivers. Often, a raiding party would come ahead of the main group. Out of the mist the longboats would suddenly appear, with Viking warriors wearing helmets decorated with horns. When death finally claimed a Viking, the body was buried with the owner's longboat. Such ships have been found in Denmark, complete with relics from the Viking times. Vikings were not just famous for their strength. They were especially well-known for their stories and legends. Many of our English words come from the Norse languages, along with the names for Wednesday, Thursday, and Friday.

Observing Patterns

1. Ten of the list words have two syllables. Make a chart with two columns. In column one write the two-syllable words that have the stress on the first syllable. In column two, write the two-syllable words with stress on the second syllable.

Stress on First Syllable	Stress on Second Syllable
áthlete	aheád

2. Write the four list words that have double consonants.

3. A comparison that shows differences is called a **contrast**. Complete each contrast below by writing a list word.

a) At first the small ship was behind the rest, but later it sailed _____ .

b) I was missing two stamps from my collection, but now it is _____ .

c) The Vikings looked _____ , but land was nowhere to be found.

4. Write the four list words that would be found in the dictionary between the words below.

dream / icicle

Discovering Patterns

ahead already death wearing instead complete supreme athlete journey hockey carry everywhere especially finally suddenly body

1. Write the five list words that have the short vowel sound /e/ as in **heaven**. Circle the letters that make this sound.

2. Many of the list words have the long vowel sound /ē/ as in **me**. The /ē/ sound can be spelled in more than one way. Write the /ē/ list words under three headings.

/ē/ spelled **e_e** as in **these**	/ē/ spelled **ey** as in **money**	/ē/ spelled **y** as in **happy**

POWERBOOSTER

- The short vowel sound /e/ is sometimes spelled **ea** as in **heaven**.
- The long vowel sound /ē/ may be spelled **e_e**, **ey**, or **y**.

Exploring Patterns

1. In each set of words below, one word contains the long vowel sound /ē/. Write the /ē/ words, but remember that /ē/ can be spelled several ways. Copy the circled letters. When they are unscrambled, they will tell how it might feel to meet a ship of Viking sailors.

a) leather   cream   heaven   ⊙_ _ _ _

b) hey   away   key   _ _⊙

c) January   May   July   _⊙_ _ _ _ _

d) they   these   away   _ _ _⊙_

e) spade   spread   speaker   _ _ _ _ _ _⊙

Unscrambled word: _ _ _ _ _

2. Combine the base words below to form as many compound words as possible.

some   thing   any   body

every   one   no   where

3. Many adverbs are formed by adding **-ly** to base words.

Example: final + **ly** = finally; late + **ly** = lately

          Notice what happens when the base word ends in **y**.

Example: happy + **ly** = happily

Copy the chart into your notebook and fill in all the spaces.

Base Word	Adverb
complete	_____
_____	suddenly
easy	_____
secret	_____
_____	greedily

4. Complete this limerick with list words that fit the shapes.

There once was a great ⬚⬚⬚⬚ team

They'd ⬚⬚⬚⬚⬚ the puck like a dream

Then ⬚⬚⬚⬚⬚ score

And go back for more.

As ⬚⬚⬚⬚⬚ **s** they all were ⬚⬚⬚⬚⬚.

5. Describe how these Viking children like being in your class. For example, how do they like playing baseball at recess or using a computer to do their work?

Challenges with Words

1. Write the Super Word that fits each blank below.

a) The Vikings were _ _ _ _ _ _ sailors and pirates.

b) By the _ _ _ _ _ _ _ _ _ _ of the Viking era, their armies had travelled across Europe.

c) A _s_ _u_ _r_ _v_ _ _ _ of English towns would show that many were first Viking settlements.

d) The sword, axe, and longbow were Viking _ _ _ _.

e) On a _ _ _ _ _ _ across the Atlantic, Viking sailors navigated by the stars and sun.

f) The Vikings are not only remembered for their _ _ _ _ _ _ _ and plunder, but for their strength and skill.

━━━━━━━━━ **WORDS IN HISTORY** ━━━━━━━━━

Some Viking words have come down to us almost unchanged. These words — **egg**, **tree**, **band**, **leg**, **race**, **take**, and **thrust** — are the same words in modern English.

2. Many English words that begin with **sk** or **sc** come from the Vikings. Write the English words for these Old Norse words.

Old Norse	English
skyrta, a long shirt	
skrap, something scraped off	
skith, a slab of wood or a snowshoe	
skraema, to cry out	

voyage
survey
fierce
robbery
weapons
completion

3. The letters **ea** make both the sound /e/ as in **weapons**, and /ē/ as in **season**. Find ten words that contain the letters **ea** and add them to the groups below.

4. The Vikings visited the islands of Iceland and Newfoundland in their travels. Imagine you are on a voyage in a Viking ship. Write a story describing your journey, using as many Super Words as you can. You may want to start your story like this:

After a **fierce** storm, we finally arrived on the island of...

5. All the new words have the /ôr/ sound. Notice that a **port** was once only a place where ships docked. The word **sportsplex** is a combination of **sports** and **plex**, which means to make a network. **Cordless** was a word that was invented when many electrical appliances and telephones no longer had cords that needed to be plugged in.

Unscramble the words in the sentences below.

a) We played hockey at the new **xtposerslp** in our neighbourhood.

b) The **rpot** on my computer allows me to connect to a printer.

c) Our **lcsosrde** phone is usually hard to find.

NEW WORDS

cordless
sportsplex
port

10

Long i
i   y   ight
pilot   style   flash**ight**

bicycle
kinds
style
bright
finds
pedal
flashlight
highway
pilot
surprising
tiny
frightened
chain
quiet
traffic
front

Exploring the World of the Bicycle

Imagine racing along a <u>bright</u>, <u>quiet</u> prairie <u>highway</u> or keeping up with the city's rush hour <u>traffic</u> on a bike path. Bicycles are an exciting way to travel. The modern bike, first called the Safety Bicycle, was developed in 1893. The Safety Bicycle replaced bikes like the High-Wheeler. This <u>bicycle</u> had a big <u>front</u> wheel and a <u>tiny</u> back wheel. It often <u>frightened</u> riders because it was hard to start and stop. The new <u>style</u> of bike was much safer. It had brakes and a <u>chain</u> which allowed the rider to <u>pedal</u> the back wheel. Today there are many <u>kinds</u> of bikes, from sturdy mountain bicycles to racers. But any bicycle can provide the rider with <u>surprising</u> adventures as it <u>finds</u> its way to places cars could never go.

Observing Patterns

1. Write the list words that fit these shapes.

2. Write the list word in which the letter **y** spells the long vowel sound /ī/ as in **tie**.

3. Write the six list words that have only one syllable.

4. Write the list word that is the opposite of **back**.

5. Unscramble the letters inside the chain and write the list words.

fifcart   apled   otlip   ytles

6. Write the two list words that are compounds.

Discovering Patterns

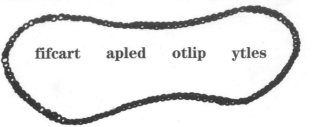

bicycle kinds style bright finds pedal flashlight highway pilot surprising tiny frightened chain quiet traffic front

1. Write the base word for **surprising**. Underline the pattern of letters in the base word that spell the sound /ī/ as in **size**.

2. Write the base word for **frightened**. Underline the letters in the base word that spell the long vowel sound /ī/.

3. There are other ways of spelling /ī/ as well. Make a chart in your notebook like the one below. Write the list words that have the sound /ī/ under the correct headings.

/ī/ spelled **i** as in **mind**	/ī/ spelled **igh** as in **sigh**	/ī/ spelled **y** as in **cycle**

Find words of your own to fit each pattern.

46

Exploring Patterns

1. Write words with the long vowel sound /ī/ by adding letters to each word part on the wheels. How many words can you create?

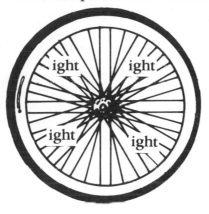 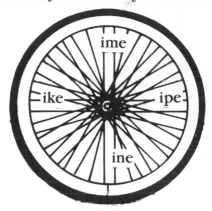

2. Complete each set of comparisons with a list word.
   a) **Bicycle** is to **bike path** as **car** is to _____ .
   b) **Bright** is to **dim** as **noisy** is to _____ .
   c) **Accelerator** is to **car** as _____ is to **bike**.
   d) **Engineer** is to **train** as _____ is to **airplane**.

3. The following pairs of words are related in meaning. One word from each pair has the sound /ī/ as in **bike**, while the other has the sound /i/ as in **kitten**. Write each sentence using the correct words for the blank spaces.

   crime   criminal   a) Someone who commits a _____ is a _____ .

   invite   invitation   b) When you _____ friends to a party you should send an _____ .

   hide   hidden   c) I found some money _____ in this jar. Did you _____ it there?

4. Illustrate each of these list words in a way that would tell something about its meaning.

   tiny   frightened   chain   highway

   Examples:

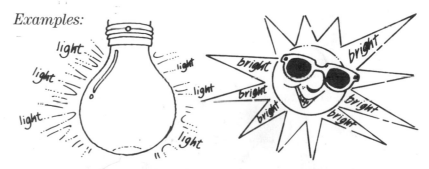

5. Cyclists must obey the law, just like motorists. Use the picture to write the rules for the cyclists. Use some of these list words in your rules.

bicycle   highway   travel   traffic

6. Make your own list of bike words. Study this list and have a partner dictate it to you. Your list might include useful words such as **spokes** or **reflectors**.

Challenges with Words

1. Write the Super Words that fit these clues.
  a) You might need this when going up hills.
  b) Don't forget to _____ your spokes.
  c) Any type of land transportation is a _____ .
  d) This is how you fix a broken part.
  e) You will need this on the rear of your bike.
  f) The athletes in this race are _____ .

2. Use the letters of the word **gearshift** to make other words. Score two points for every word you make with two letters, three points for every three-letter word, and so on. How far can you get on the race track?

tighten
cyclists
~~**vehicle**~~
reflector
gearshift last
repair

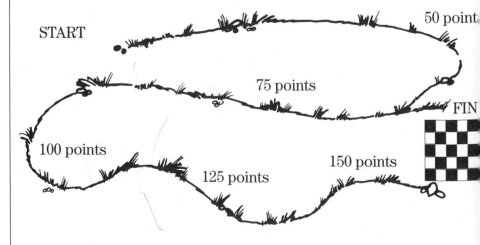

START

50 point

75 points

FIN

100 points

125 points

150 points

48

ANNUAL SPRING BIKE RACE

3. Keep your 'i's on this thrilling race! Use words with the long vowel sound /ī/ to fill in the blanks. Then finish the story with your own words. Use as many 'i' words as you can.

It was a terrifying **(igh)** to see my brother Kevin **(i_e)** into the wall on the turn. Luckily, he suffered only a **(igh)** scrape on his leg, but his glasses were broken in his fall. We all gave a huge **(igh)** of relief when he rode over the finish **(i_e)**. He was not **(i_e)** last—just **(i)** out of ten riders. I was just glad to see him **(i_e)**!....

━━━━━━━━ **WORDS IN HISTORY** ━━━━━━━━

The word **cycle** probably came from the word kyklos, which meant a 'ring' or 'circle' in ancient Greek. It was later used to mean anything which moved in a circle—like the wheel of a bicycle.

4. How many parts of a bicycle can you name? Draw a picture of a bicycle and label its parts with the names you know. Then check an encyclopedia or picture dictionary for more part names and correct spellings.

5. Make your own **vehicle** crossword. With a partner, list all the types of vehicles you know. Then write definitions for each one and make a crossword puzzle to try on your friends.

		²b		
¹t	r	u	c	k
		s		

11

Vowels with r

serve   fur   worked

people
muscle
gentle
example
serve
purring
handle
herself
furry
worked
greatly
swiftly
silently
whiskers
quietly
worst

Exploring the History of Cats

One day, more than 5000 years ago, a small striped animal with <u>whiskers</u> walked <u>silently</u> into the fields of an Egyptian farmer. It was the African wildcat, and the farmer let it stay to catch mice and rats. The arrangement <u>worked</u> well, for rodents were one of the <u>worst</u> problems facing farmers in Egypt, and the cat could kill them <u>swiftly</u> and <u>quietly</u>. After a thousand years the wildcat became <u>gentle</u> and easy to <u>handle</u>. It was <u>greatly</u> loved by the <u>people</u> of Egypt and even thought of as a god. This Egyptian cat was the first <u>example</u> of the present-day house cat. Today's cats <u>serve</u> us more as pets than rodent catchers. What could be more peaceful than a <u>furry</u> ball, <u>purring</u> <u>herself</u> to sleep in your lap? With every <u>muscle</u> relaxed, it is hard to imagine that this cat was once a fierce wildcat of Africa.

Observing Patterns

1. Write the five list words that end in the letters **le**.

2. Complete the list words on each paw.

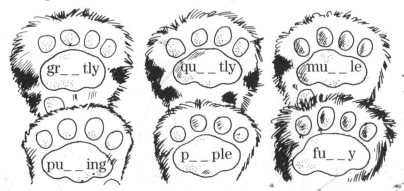

gr_ _ tly   qu_ _ tly   mu_ _ le

pu_ _ ing   p_ _ ple   fu_ _ y

3. Write the list words that mean the opposite of these words.

rough best slowly himself

4. Write the six list words that would be found in the dictionary between the words shown below. Hint! You need to look at the third letter in the word **would**.

sample / would

5. Unscramble the list words. The circled letters should tell you what clouds are:

ferselh _ _ _ _ _ _ ◯
legent _ _ _ _ ◯ _
rupginr _ ◯ _ _ _ _ _
rufry ◯ _ _ _ _
ylfiwst _ _ _ ◯ _ _ _
lqieuyt _ _ _ _ _ ◯
Unscrambled word: _ _ _ _ _ _

Discovering Patterns

people muscle gentle example serve purring handle herself furry worked greatly swiftly silently whiskers quietly worst.

1. Seven of the list words have the sound /ėr/ as in **dirt**. Make a chart like the one below in your notebook. Write the list words that have the sound /ėr/ under the correct headings.

/ėr/ spelled **er** as in **under**	/ėr/ spelled **ur** as in **curly**	/ėr/ spelled **or** as in **worm**

2. Write the list words that end in **-ly**. Underline the base word for each.

POWERBOOSTER

- The sound /ėr/ is sometimes spelled **er** as in **her**, **ur** as in **curly**, or **or** as in **worm**.
- The suffix **-ly** may be added to many base words.

Exploring Patterns

1. Find the correct letter in each part of the puzzle. Then unscramble the letters to spell a breed of cat.

    a) This letter is in **purred** but not in **drummer**.

    b) This letter is in **furry** but not in **funny**.

    c) This letter is in **quieter** but not in **quarter**.

    d) This letter is in **worst** but not in **worth**.

    e) This letter is in **earn** but not in **fear**.

    f) This letter is in **great** but not in **greeting**.

    g) This letter is in **muscle** but not in **muscular**.

This type of cat makes a good house pet. _ _ _ _ _ _ _

2. Read the dictionary entry for the word **serve**.

serve   (sèrv) **1** be a servant **2** put food or drink on the table **3** supply enough for **4** in tennis and similar games, put the ball in play by hitting it.

Copy each sentence, then write the number of the dictionary meaning that matches it.

    a) One pie will serve six people.

    b) He served as a butler in the old mansion.

    c) She served the ball so hard that I couldn't return it.

    d) The waiter served us our meal.

3. 'Tom Swifties' are jokes that use adverbs to create puns. For example:

"I hate February," he said **coldly**. Complete each 'Tom Swifty' using one of the adverbs in the box. Write the sentences.

    a) "This lemon is sour," she complained _____ .

    b) "Don't touch the knife," her mother warned _____ .

    c) "This box is only one kilogram," she said _____ .

    d) "The storm is finally over," he announced _____ .

4. Write your own expressions about cats. Use some of these list words: **silently**, **swiftly**, **quietly**, **furry**, **whiskers**.

Example: She walks as _____ as a cat.

Can you think of other 'Tom Swifties'?

lightly
calmly
bitterly
sharply

5. There are lots of expressions or **idioms** about cats. Use each of these idioms in a sentence or two that explains what you think they mean.

    a) raining cats and dogs
    b) looks like something the cat dragged in
    c) curiosity killed the cat
    d) let the cat out of the bag
    e) cat nap

Challenges with Words

1. Write the Super Words that are synonyms for the underlined words below.

The night wind howled through the thick forest. The jaguar moved <u>smoothly</u> from tree to tree in search of food. It was a <u>clever</u> and skilful hunter. Its quivering muscles were ready to <u>dive</u> on anything moving on the jungle floor. Suddenly it spied two small, glowing eyes. It plunged down into the darkness, ready to <u>grapple</u> with its surprised prey. Quickly the jaguar would <u>eat</u> up its meal, then <u>sluggishly</u> steal off to a sheltered tree for a rest.

2. How many different words can you find that are synonyms for **gobble**? Use the chart below to match syllables and make three such words. Then think of three more of your own.

swal	vour
con	low
de	sume

intelligent
gracefully
gobble
wrestle
lazily
pounce

3. Many words in English end in **-le** or **-ly**. **Ly** is a suffix we add to the end of many words. **Le** is part of the word. Match the **-le** and **-ly** words in the box to the spaces below.

    a) **Knapsack** is to **strap** as **cup** is to _____ .

    b) **Tall** is to **short** as **selfishly** is to _____ .

    c) **Adult** is to **bed** as **baby** is to _____ .

    d) **Jet** is to **noisily** as **panther** is to _____ .

    e) **Elephant** is to **heavily** as **mouse** is to _____ .

    f) **Water** is to **clear** as **handwriting** is to _____ .

4. How smart do you think you are? Use the letters in the Super Word **intelligent** to make as many short words as you can. Score one point for each letter.

I N T E L L I G E N T

5. Help! Mortimer is turning into a CAT! His fingernails are becoming claws. He's sprouting whiskers and stripes. The question is—will he be a nice tame little pussycat or a fierce tiger? Write a story about Mortimer's experience and what will happen next. Use as many Super Words in your story as you can.

6. There are some interesting new words from the field of communications. Write the words that fit these sentences.

    a) She communicates with friends around the world on the _____ .

    b) Today I had six messages on my _____ _____ .

    c) He turned on the _____ so everyone in the room could hear the conversation.

WORDS

voice mail

Internet

speakerphone

STUDY STEPS

LOOK
SAY
COVER
WRITE
CHECK

Here is a list of words that may have been hard for you in Units 7–11. You and your teacher may add other words to the list.

desert	eastern	everywhere	quiet
worst	Arctic	especially	frightened
earliest	wearing	finally	surprising
against	journey	bicycle	muscle

1. Use the Study Steps for each word. Your teacher will dictate the words.

2. Complete the story with words from the Study List. Write the story in your notebook.

My first long j _ _ r n _ _ by b _ c _ c _ _ was part of a 'Bike-a-thon' for charity. I was one of the _ _ r l _ e s t to arrive, and was f r _ e n _ _ that I might not be able to keep up. It was the w _ _ s t day of the fall, and we had to ride _ g _ _ n s t a cold wind that seemed to come from the A _ t _ ! Soon there were bikes e v _ _ _ where with riders w _ _ r i n g gloves, hats, and scarves. All was q _ _ _ t and peaceful when we f i n _ _ _ y began our ride through the _ _ s t _ _ n part of the country. It was s _ _ p r _ _ i n g how I kept up with the others, _ special _ _ since every m u _ _ _ _ in my body was aching! When I was finally back home, I promised myself that my next 'Bike-a-thon' would be across a nice hot d _ _ _ _ t!

3. Unscramble the syllables to make words on the Study List.

pris sur ing   ry where eve

pe ly es cial   li est ear

4. Remember that a **common noun** names a person, place, or thing. A **proper noun** is a special name, always written with a capital letter. Complete the following sentences with the correct common or proper nouns.

a) I collected some information about the Sahara _____ .
I had not realized that a _____ may contain streams of water beneath the sand. (desert/Desert)

b) Just as we take care of the _____ in our gardens we also need to protect our planet _____ (earth/Earth)

c) A cold _____ air mass moved south from the _____ Circle. (arctic/Arctic)

5. Sort the words below into the following categories.

    a) /ėr/ spelled **er** as in **her**
    b) /ėr/ spelled **ir** as in **dirt**
    c) /ėr/ spelled **ur** as in **turn**
    d) /ėr/ spelled **ear** as in **early**
    e) /ėr/ spelled **or** as in **work**

search	certain	world	circle	surname
worth	birthday	earth	worst	herself
purple	service	surface	earliest	third

6. Complete the following sentences with one of the words below. Sometimes more than one word will fit.

greatly   quietly   swiftly   silently

    a) The parents talked _____ because the baby was asleep.
    b) The river flowed _____ as it neared the rapids.
    c) The cat waited _____ for the mouse to appear.
    d) Your skating has improved _____ since you began taking lessons.

7. Write sentences using these **-ly** words.

suddenly   finally   brightly   gently

8. Write the word from each set that fits the clues in the brackets.

    a) journey style tiny   (/ī/ spelled **y** as in **cycle**)
    b) death hear better   (/e/ spelled **ea** as in **heaven**)
    c) horse worth north   (/ėr/ spelled **or** as in **work**)
    d) warm barely darkness   (/är/ pelled **ar** as in **large**)

9. The following words contain letters which are not clearly sounded. Write each word and highlight these letters in some way. For example, print them in large letters, use a different colour ink, or underline them.

Example: Seas**O**n

Arctic   **muscle**   **surprising**   **everywhere**   **frightened**

Make your own review list, and use the five study steps.

Dictionary Skills

1. **Using a Spelling Chart:** A spelling chart in a dictionary gives the common spellings of English sounds. It can help you spell words you do not know.

   Study the part of the spelling chart shown below.

Common Spelling of English Sounds	
Sound	**Spelling**
/ī/	**ai**sle, **ei**ther, **eye**, **i**ce, h**igh**
/g/	**g**o, **gh**ost, **gu**ess
/h/	**h**e, **wh**o
/m/	**m**e, cli**mb**ing, sole**mn**
/n/	**gn**aw, **kn**ife, **n**ut
/r/	**r**un, **rh**ythm, **wr**ong
/s/	**c**ent, **ps**alm, **s**ay, **sc**ience, **sw**ord

   a) In what ways can the consonant sound /s/ be spelled at the beginning of words?
   b) In what ways is /ī/ spelled at the beginning of words?
   c) In what ways is the /n/ sound spelled at the beginning of words?
   d) In what ways is the /h/ sound spelled at the beginning of words?

2. Look at the words below. If you did not know how to spell them, how would you use the chart to help find them in a dictionary? Write the word from the spelling chart that would help you find the correct spelling in the dictionary.

scene	write	circle	bright
guide	whole	knew	thumb

Exploring Ways to Travel

1. There are many exciting ways to travel. Make a chart such as the one below for three different ways of travelling. Under each heading write the type of vehicle, what makes it move, and where it is used.

	Bicycling	Canoeing	Flying
vehicle			airplane
motion		paddles	
place	land		

2. What's your favourite method of travelling? Write a brief paragraph about the way you like to travel. Explain why it's your favourite method.

3. Have you ever thought about time travel? With a group or partner choose a time either in the future or the past. Imagine what a visit to that time would be like. Write a story about your time travel.

Grammar Power

1. Writing with Adjectives: Adjectives describe, or modify, nouns. A dog isn't just a dog. It can be big and hairy, or thin and yappy. Here are some adjectives from Units 1–12.

difficult	**huge**	**cheap**	**solid**	**blue**
bright	**tiny**	**quiet**	**gentle**	**furry**

Find a noun to go with each adjective above. Write a phrase.

Example: *a solid chocolate*

2. Making Comparisons: You can use adjectives to compare two persons or things. For example, suppose you want to compare an elephant to a mouse. If the adjective is a short word like big, add **-er**. If it is a long word like lovable, then use **more** before the adjective.

Example: *The elephant is **bigger** than a mouse.*

Complete these comparisons:
a) An elephant is **quieter** than _____ .
b) An elephant is **smaller** than _____ .
c) An elephant is **more lovable** than _____ .
d) An elephant is **more expensive** than _____ .

3. Using Superlatives: You can also use adjectives to compare more than two persons or things. If the adjective is a short word like fast, add **-est**. If it is a long word like experienced, then use **most** before the adjective.

Example: *You are the **fastest** swimmer of the six team members.*
*She is the **most experienced** player in the class.*

Complete these superlatives with your own ideas.
a) I think the **greatest** baseball player in the world is _____ .
b) I think the **tallest** building in the world is _____ .
c) I think the **most beautiful** view in the world is _____ .
d) I think the **most delicious** food in the world is _____ .

"Why are an elephant's ankles more wrinkled than a giraffe's? Because elephants wear their running shoes too tight."

Look in a thesaurus to find lots of synonyms. Sometimes antonyms are listed too.

4. Synonyms are words that mean the same or almost the same thing. **Antonyms** mean the opposite.

   a) Find two synonyms for each adjective in the chart below.

Adjective	Synonym
huge	
gentle	
bright	

   b) Find antonyms for the adjectives in the chart below.

Adjective	Antonym
cheap	
difficult	
quiet	

Proofing Power

Read the following paragraph, looking for errors. List the words you think are misspelled, giving their correct spelling.

Last night I had a dream that I was riding around the world on my bicicle. I was ridding agianst the wind, and everything else was quite. I was waring my favourite pair of overalls that were perfect for the jerney. I rode everywere: in the dessert, in the artic, in the mountains. It is surprising how much mussle it takes to ride a bike! Sometimes, esecially in the most earlyest morning hours, I was frigtened that I might not make it home. But I kept going. When I was in easturn Canada, they had the wesrt storm I had ever seen. Finaly, I made it home. Was I exhausted!

13

Long o
o ow
hold   slowly

hold
motor
notice
robot
follow
growing
known
slowly
throw
furniture
adventures
picture
future
spaceship
travel
during

Exploring the World of Space Travel

5....4....3....2....1....<u>hold</u> onto your seat....blast off! From make-believe to moon flights, the idea of <u>travel</u> by <u>spaceship</u> has always interested people. Can you <u>picture</u> what it would be like to <u>follow</u> the paths of the stars? <u>Slowly</u> your spacecraft leaves Earth. The rocket <u>motor</u> is pushing you up through the sky. <u>During</u> takeoff, you have been so busy you didn't <u>notice</u> your planet <u>growing</u> smaller and smaller behind you. Soon it will disappear completely. Giant <u>robot</u> arms put heat shields into place. They will <u>throw</u> off the sun's dangerous rays. Now you can settle back into your chair. Like all the <u>furniture</u> on board, it has been specially designed. What <u>future</u> <u>adventures</u> are waiting for you are not <u>known</u>. But whatever they are, you and your spaceship will be ready.

Observing Patterns

1. Write the eleven list words that have two syllables. Put a mark over the syllable that is stressed.

2. Unscramble the syllables on each rocket to form a list word.

ni fur ture

tures ven ad

59

Synonyms mean the same. Antonyms mean the opposite.

3. Write the list words that mean almost the same as the words below.

grasp   engine   journey

4. Write the list words that mean the opposite of these words.

shrinking   catch   past   lead

5. Write the two list words that begin with the sound /n/. Underline the letter or letters that spell the /n/ sound in each word.

6. Write the two list words that would be found in the dictionary between the words below.

snowball / told

Discovering Patterns

hold motor notice robot follow growing known slowly throw furniture adventures picture future spaceship travel during

1. Write the list words that have the sound /ch/ as in **nature**. Underline the parts of these words that are the same.

2. Many of the list words have the long **o** sound as in **old** and **blow**. Write the /ō/ list words under two headings.

/ō/ spelled **o** as in **old**	/ō/ spelled **ow** as in **blow**

POWERBOOSTER

- The long vowel sound /ō/ may be spelled **o** as in **old** or **ow** as in **blow**.
- In some words the /cher/ sound follows the pattern -**ture** as in **nature**.

Exploring Patterns

1. Program the word memory of the robot with words that have the long **o** sound spelled **ow** as in **blow**. Use at least five of these words in sentences.

2. Complete this story with list words. Write the story in your notebook.

If you could step into the _____ , what do you think you would see? Perhaps you would _____ from planet to planet by _____ . An electronic _____ would help you _____ your visit and would _____ you on all your _____ . You would probably _____ that chairs, beds, and other _____ were very different from today. Draw a _____ of the future as you think it might be.

3. A word web contains words and phrases that go with the word in the centre.

Example:

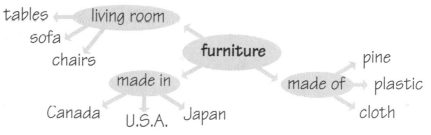

Make a word web for two of these list words.

spaceship   future   travel

4. Complete each puzzle with a rhyming list word. Write the pairs of rhyming words.

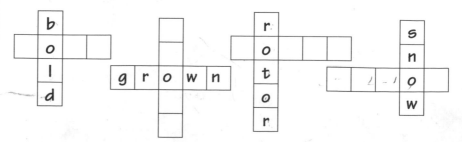

5. Your travel agency is selling seats on a tour of the planets. Design a poster to attract customers for this exciting trip to Mars, Jupiter, Saturn, Mercury, Pluto, Venus, Uranus, and Neptune. Use some of these list words on your poster.

travel   adventures   future   spaceship

Check your poster carefully to make sure you've included all the important information about the tour.

Challenges with Words

1. Use the Super Words to complete the radio message below.

Radio Log. Moon City. April 25, 2145
From: Landing Module, Captain Isaacs
Message: Completed our _____ landing at 1500 hours. Two
crew members suffered slight _____ sickness but since
landing there have been no _____ health problems. Just
before landing, spacecraft was _____ to high levels of
_____ radiation. Expect our _____ date to be May 3 or 4.

2. a) The following words all have something to do with space travel. Write an antonym or opposite for each word.

launch   enormous   motion   freezing   survive
automatic   distant   breathable   approach   known

b) Write five more words that describe space travel, then write antonyms for your words.

Super Words

lunar
motion
exposed
cosmic
departure
noticeable

Lunar comes from the Latin word <u>luna</u>, meaning 'moon'. Our word lunatic comes from this root. (The Romans believed that the moon could affect peoples' minds and make them mad.)

Can you think of a reason why noticeable keeps its e?

3. **Cosmic** comes from the ancient Greek language. Use your dictionary to write the meaning of **cosmic**. What other words can you find that are related to **cosmic**?

4. What can you see? Starting with each letter of **noticeable**, write a word that names something you see every day. Score one point for each letter. A score of over 70 is very good.

Example:

N	O	T	I	C	E	A	B	L	E
o	r	e							
s	a	l							
e	n	e							
	g	p							
	e	h							
		o							
		n							
		e							

5. a) Make words by combining the syllables below with **-ture**.

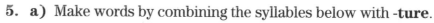

lec   frac   crea   depar   na   signa   pic

b) Choose three of the words you made in a) and write sentences of your own.

6. Use as many Super Words as you can to complete this radio transmission from the surface of the moon.

Mission Control: Pluto, this is Mission Control. Do you read? Over.

Pluto: Mission Control this is Pluto. Go ahead with your transmission. Over.

Mission Control: Pluto, we need to relay your departure time to the lunar orbiting station. A problem has developed and we........

NEW WORDS

robotics

modem

e–mail

7. Write the new words that fit these clues.

_____ is the science of using robots.

_____ is the short form for electronic mail.

_____ is the name for a device that sends computer information across telephone lines.

14 Plurals
matches   planets

spirals
addresses
telescope
kilometres
matches
states
branches
arms
coaches
bunches
waves
classes
objects
groups
directions
planets

Exploring the Galaxies

On a black, moonless night, if a person watches the sky carefully, he or she may see small, bright fuzzy <u>objects</u>. Scientists using powerful telescopes can see that these objects are really <u>bunches</u> of stars. These <u>groups</u> of billions and billions of stars are called galaxies. Like <u>planets</u> around the sun, the stars in a galaxy pass around its centre, travelling trillions of <u>kilometres</u> in each year. Our own sun is part of a galaxy called the Milky Way. It <u>matches</u> a type of galaxy known as a spiral galaxy. This looks like a flattened disc with long curved <u>branches</u> or <u>arms</u>. These arms or <u>spirals</u> are made up of young stars in various <u>states</u> of evolution. Thanks to the radio <u>telescope</u>, which receives electro magnetic <u>waves</u> from space, many more <u>classes</u> of galaxies have been discovered. There are so many that they have been given special names and <u>addresses</u> on our star charts.

Observing Patterns

1. Complete the list words on each star.

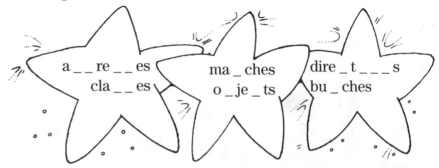

a _ _ re _ _ es
cla _ _ es

ma _ ches
o _ je _ ts

dire _ t _ _ _ s
bu _ ches

2. The word part -**scope** means an instrument for viewing or observing. Write the list word that contains -**scope**. Explain how this word fits with the meaning of -**scope**.

3. Write the list word that belongs with each set. Add a word of your own to each set.

    a) stars   comets   moons   _____

    b) shoulders   hands   fingers   _____

    c) millimetres   centimetres   metres   _____

    d) players   trainers   referees   _____

    e) roots   trunks   leaves   _____

4. Write the list words that rhyme with these words. Underline the letters that spell the rhyming sounds.

        waits   alarms   behaves   stoops

Discovering Patterns

spirals addresses telescope kilometres matches states branches arms coaches bunches waves classes objects groups directions planets

1. Complete the chart with list words that end in the sound **-es** as in **glasses**. Write the singular form of each word. What sounds are at the end of these base words?

Plural	Singular
glasses	glass

2. Write the plural list words that end in the sound /s/ or /z/ as in **suits** and **caves**. Underline the singular form of each word.

65

Exploring Patterns

1. Make a list of the objects in outer space that you might see with a powerful telescope. In one column, write the singular form of the word, then in the second column write the plural.

Example: **Singular**   **Plural**
         planet   planets

2. Many of the list words can be used as either nouns or verbs.

Example: *That plant has many tiny <u>branches</u>.*
          This road <u>branches</u> off in three directions.

Use each of these list words in two sentences—first as a noun, then as a verb.

waves   coaches

3. Complete this story with the list words that fit the shapes below. Write the story in your notebook.

For our scavenger hunt, the ⬚⬚⬚⬚⬚ were broken

into five ⬚⬚⬚⬚. We were given

⬚⬚⬚⬚⬚⬚ for finding several

⬚⬚⬚⬚⬚⬚, and at each place we had to

locate certain ⬚⬚⬚⬚. We ended up walking

about five ⬚⬚⬚⬚⬚ but we found

everything on the list!

4. Write these list words so that their shape tells something about their meaning.

waves   directions   planets   spirals

Example:

₉ r o w i n g

5. A space probe is being sent out into the universe to try to contact other life forms. You have been asked to send a message as a young person from Earth. Describe yourself to an alien who has never met a young human being. You may want to use an outline for a space message something like this:

My name is _____
I move by _____
I need _____
I like _____
I fear _____

Be sure to proofread your message for spelling and punctuation. When you've finished your outline, you may wish to tape your message.

Challenges with Words

1. Find the right Super Words to complete the blanks.
a) Scientists who study distant _____ with the aid of powerful telescopes are called _____ .
b) Space probes conduct _____ for intelligent life in the _____ .
c) The nearest star outside our solar system is many _____ away.

2. a) Write your own sentence using the Super Word that was left out in exercise 1.
b) Write three more words that end in **x** and add **-es** to make the plural form.

searches ✓
galaxies ✓
astronomers ✓
taxes ✓
universe ✓
light-years

The Ancient Greek word for **star** was <u>aster</u> or <u>astron</u>. From this word comes our word **astronomer**.

3. Use the code below to discover other words that come from the Greek roots <u>aster</u> and <u>astron</u>. Be careful. Extra letters have been added at the beginning and end of some words.

z y x w t q m l k j i h g f d c b s u p e r n o v a
A B C D E F G H I J K L M N O P Q R S T U V W X Y Z

    a) ozupsdfxepz   **b)** zszupsdhdmv   **c)** zuptskuihg
    d) pzzuptsdkwb   **e)** zupsdfdgv   **f)** lkzupsdfdgkxzh

4. Write the plural forms of these words. Some are tricky, so check your dictionary for irregular plurals.

    a) blush   **b)** hostess   **c)** zoo
    d) galaxy   **e)** chief   **f)** hero
    g) shelf   **h)** waltz   **i)** wretch

5. Verbs that end in **ch**, **sh**, **ss**, **zz**, and **z** also add **-es**.

Example: *The light **flashes** on and off.*

Use a verb that ends in **-es** to complete these sentences.

    a) She _____ her dog. **b)** He _____ on a star.
    c) The bee _____ .   **d)** The runner _____ 100 metres.

6. Write your own sentences with these verbs.
        crunches   crushes   tosses   fizzes

7. A **light year** is the distance light travels in one year. That's about 9 500 000 000 000 (9.5 trillion) kilometres! Use a book or a CD-ROM to research astronomy and complete the space chart below. You may want to add other planets, galaxies, nebulas, or quasars to the list.

OBJECTS IN SPACE		
Name	**Type**	**Distance from Earth**
Mars	planet	78 000 000 km
Andromeda	galaxy	
Neptune		
Venus		
Milky Way		

Irregular Plurals

berries   knives

List words:

berries
usually
enemies
mountain
grizzlies
digging
largest
knives
deer
America
bones
wives
camper
bees
lives
become

Exploring the World of Grizzlies

The wild and rugged mountain wilderness of North America is home to the grizzly bear. Grizzlies have no natural enemies except humans. They usually live peaceful lives digging under rocks for ants, tearing apart stumps to get at the honey that wild bees have stored, catching fish, and eating wild berries. The problem is that grizzlies can become dangerous if a camper leaves behind garbage, and they get used to eating human food. Although grizzlies are not the largest bears on this continent, they have claws like knives and can break bones with one swipe of their mighty paws. As the wilderness shrinks, it's important to remember that moose, deer, bears, and many other large animals need a place where their lives are not disturbed by contact with people.

Observing Patterns

1. Write the four list words that have double consonants, and the two list words that have double vowels. Underline the double letters in each word.

2. Complete the following comparisons with list words.
   a) **Stirring** is to **spoons** as **cutting** is to _____ .
   b) **Pond** is to **lake** as **hill** is to _____ .
   c) **Lightest** is to **heaviest** as **smallest** is to _____ .
   d) **Tree** is to **wood** as **skeleton** is to _____ .

3. Write the three one-syllable list words that rhyme.

4. Write list words by unscrambling the syllables on the caves.

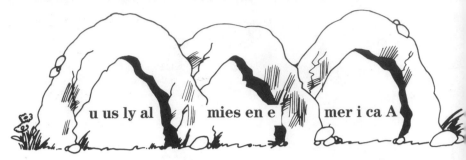

u us ly al   mies en e   mer i ca A

5. Complete the sets with a list word that has the same spelling pattern.

a) cheer	steer	_____
b) damper	hamper	_____
c) stones	telephones	_____
d) captain	fountain	_____
e) trees	knees	_____
f) welcome	handsome	_____

Hint!
Look for the rhyming pattern at the ends of the words.

Discovering Patterns

*berries usually enemies mountain grizzlies
digging largest knives deer America
bones wives camper bees lives become*

1. Write the singular forms of these plural list words.

knives   wives   lives

What change is made to the singular when the plural is formed?

2. Write the singular forms of these plural words.

berries   grizzlies   enemies

What change is made to the word when the plural is formed?

3. Which list word is spelled the same in the singular and the plural form?

POWERBOOSTER

- Words that have the pattern **ife** as in **life** form the plural by changing the **f** to **v** and adding -**s**.
- Words that end in a consonant plus **y** such as **story** form the plural by changing **y** to **i** and adding -**es**.

Exploring Patterns

1. Write the plural forms of the words shown on the bear tracks.

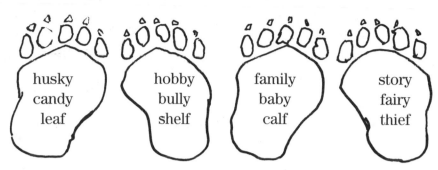

| husky
candy
leaf | hobby
bully
shelf | family
baby
calf | story
fairy
thief |

Choose any four of the plural words you have made, and write a sentence that has an interesting sound.

2. These words are all related in meaning:

usual   usually   unusual

Write the words that fit the sentences below.

a) The fur of a grizzly bear is _____ tipped with white.

b) The _____ diet of grizzlies is rodents, fish, and berries.

c) Because of their great size and long, straight claws, it is _____ for grizzlies to climb trees.

3. Change the underlined words in the paragraph to their plural form, then rewrite the paragraph.

The <u>camper</u> took a <u>knife</u> with <u>her</u> when <u>she</u> went camping in the mountains. When <u>she</u> first spotted the <u>grizzly</u>, the bear was munching on a <u>berry</u>. The <u>woman</u> had to run for <u>her</u> <u>life</u> because the <u>grizzly</u> thought <u>she</u> was an <u>enemy</u>.

4. Make a list of all the kinds of berries you can think of. Add the ideas of your classmates to your list.

5. Is a cherry a berry? Why or why not? Check the definition of **berry** in your dictionary to help with your answer.

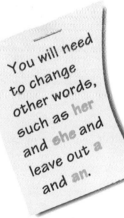

You will need to change other words, such as *her* and *she* and leave out *a* and *an*.

6. Describe your feelings as you and your friends come around the corner of a mountain trail and meet this grizzly! Use as many of these words as you can.

mountain   usually   largest   camper

7. The word **bear** rhymes with an amazing number of other words. With a partner, brainstorm as many rhyming words as you can. You might want to write a nonsense poem with your rhyming word list. It could start something like this:

> There was a young grizzly bear
> Who tried to have lunch with the mayor...

Challenges with Words

1. Use the Super Words in the story below.

Grizzlies, like most bears, are often called the thieves of the _____ . After a long winter rest (some bears don't really _____), they are very hungry. In some ___C___ areas, when _____ and other food supplies are scarce, the bears go looking for food of all _____ in garbage dumps. Stay away from these grizzlies! They can cause serious _____ with one swipe of their paws.

2. In some of these words the letter **l** is not pronounced. Write the words and underline the silent **l**'s.

salmon	salty	calm	should	fault
palm	almond	film	false	walking

salmon
injuries
wilderness
conservation
hibernate
varieties

3. Write the plural forms for all the words in the forest. Then sort them into groups and say how the plural for each group is formed.

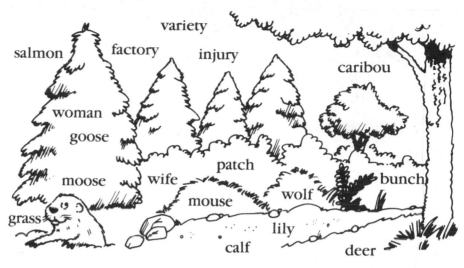

salmon factory variety injury caribou woman goose moose wife patch mouse wolf bunch grass lily calf deer

4. Here are six words that describe the wilderness. Write a synonym for each word.

silent   untamed   vacant   lovely   hazardous   deserted

5. List six of your own words to describe bears. Write synonyms for your words.

6. One meaning for the Super Word **conservation** is 'the protection and management of forests, rivers, and wildlife'. Write a paragraph about what conservation means to you. Choose one of the topics below or make up your own. Look at the Super Words to help you get ideas.
- Animals need wilderness areas untouched by people.
- Wilderness areas are important for people as well as animals.

7. The new words are all things that are handy to eat on a trip to the woods. Write the words that fit each sentence.
a) Packets of _____ food are handy on a camping trip.
b) She carried _____ _____ in her pocket as emergency snacks.
c) Our _____ _____ spilled all over the inside of my knapsack.

granola bars
freeze-dried
trail mix

73

Syllables and Stress

spécial   discóvered

discovered
instruments
carefully
interested
special
beginning
science
information
dangerous
exploring
geography
pollution
diver
least
locked
treasures

Exploring Under the Sea

People have always been underlined{interested} in the underlined{treasures} which lie under the sea. Some search for gold or silver underlined{locked} in a sunken ship. Others look for valuable mineral deposits and oil. The underlined{beginning} of serious deep-sea exploration was 100 years ago when telegraph cables were first laid across the Atlantic Ocean. Recently, underwater underlined{science} has been devoted to underlined{carefully exploring} and mapping the underlined{geography} of the ocean floor. Scientists have underlined{discovered} underwater mountain ranges, deep trenches, and underlined{information} about the underlined{least} known forms of life—bottom feeding fish. While it is underlined{dangerous} for a underlined{diver} to descend too deeply, underlined{special} diving compartments and underlined{instruments} have been invented to make exploration safer. Unfortunately, in recent years scientists have discovered that underlined{pollution} is a problem in the oceans.

Observing Patterns

1. Write the list words that have **-ed** and **-ing** endings. Underline the base word in each.

2. Write the list words that mean the opposite of these words.

ordinary   carelessly   safe   most

3. Write the three list words that would be found in the dictionary between these words.

region / universe

4. Unscramble the syllables on the shipwreck to make four list words.

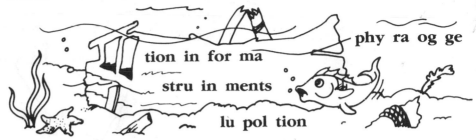

5. Write the list words that have double consonants.

Discovering Patterns

discovered instruments carefully interested special beginning science information dangerous exploring geography pollution diver least locked treasures

1. Draw four columns in your notebook, add the headings below, then write the list words under the correct heading.

one syllable	two syllables	three syllables	four syllables

2. a) Listen to where the stress is placed in the words with three syllables. Write the three-syllable words that have the stress placed on the first syllable. Put a stress mark over the first syllable.

Example: súddenly

b) Write the three-syllable words that have the stress placed on the second syllable. Put a stress mark over the second syllable.

Example: recóver

POWERBOOSTER

- In words of more than one syllable, stress is placed on only one of the syllables.

Exploring Patterns

1. Write each sentence using the word from the box that matches the clue in brackets.

a) The divers discovered valuable _____ in the shipwreck. (a word with 4 syllables)

> treasures   information

b) I am interested in reading books about _____ . (a word with stress on the first syllable)

> science   geography

c) Exploring the ocean bottom can be _____ . (a 3-syllable word with stress on the first syllable)

> exciting   dangerous   risky

2. The suffixes **-tion** or **-ation** are often added to verbs to create nouns.

Example: **pollute** *(verb)* **pollution** *(noun)*
inform *(verb)* **information** *(noun)*

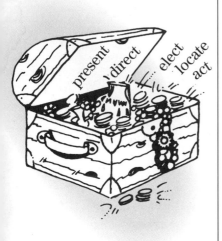

a) Change the verbs in the treasure chest to nouns by adding **-tion** or **-ation**.
b) Use each noun you have created in a sentence of your own.

3. The words **science**, **scientist**, and **scientific** are all related in meaning. Complete each sentence with the correct word.

a) The _____ used special instruments to measure the level of pollution.
b) My favourite subject in school is _____ .
c) Many important _____ discoveries have been made in recent years.

4. Add the missing letters for each list word on the whale.

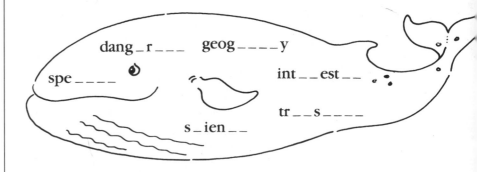

76

5. Check your instruments! You're going down 3000 metres to the bottom of the sea. Write a few sentences about what is going on in your submersible vessel. Use some of these list words in your sentences.

diver   instruments   carefully   interested

6. Imagine that you have discovered a new kind of sea creature at the bottom of an ocean trench. Describe your imaginary creature. Remember, it lives in total darkness and under the enormous pressure of the sea water.

Challenges with Words

1. Use the Super Words in the following sentences.

a) It is important to study ___e___ in order to understand how animals survive in the wild.

b) Salmon is both a ___M___ and a freshwater fish.

c) During springtime river ___c___ often wash away soil from river banks.

d) A submarine is a ___S___ boat or ship.

e) Deep sea ___T___ have been found in parts of the ocean.

f) Petroleum is a naturally ___O___ form of oil.

**marine
occurring
currents
ecology
submersible
trenches**

Add some of these 'sub' words to your personal list.

2. Sub- is a prefix meaning 'under' or 'below'. Using all the letters below only once, make five words which go with the prefix **sub-**. Each meaning is given in brackets.

aaa c dd eeee g iii mm n rrr tt v w y

a) sub _ _ _ (an underground train)
b) sub _ _ _ _ _ (take away)
c) sub _ _ _ _ _ (put under water)
d) sub _ _ _ _ _ _ (a boat that can go under water)
e) sub _ _ _ _ _ _ (divide into smaller parts)

What other words can you write that have the prefix **sub-**?

3. a) **Double Trouble**! Use the rules below to help you decide when to double the final **r** when adding **-ed**. All the base words end i one vowel and one consonant.

Rule 1: Double the final consonant if a two-syllable word has the stress on the second syllable.

Example: *preférped* + ***ed*** = *preférred*

Rule 2: Do not double the final consonant if a two-syllable word has the accent on the first syllable.

Example: *gáther* + ***ed*** = *gáthered*

- bother + ed = _____
- offer + ed = _____
- occur + ed = _____
- refer + ed = _____
- enter + ed = _____

b) Can you find three more words that follow each rule?

4. Write a story about what an ocean fish might think about human underwater exploration. Try to use as many of the Super Words as you can. A title for your story might be *A Fish-Eye's View*.

Unstressed Vowel Capital Letters

Manitoba

photograph
possible
famous
Calgary
Manitoba
station
amount
oil
beneath
area
Canada
reason
Alberta
continent
millions
country

Exploring for New Oil Fields

A lot of the gas and <u>oil</u> we buy at a gas <u>station</u>, comes from western <u>Canada</u>. <u>Calgary</u>, <u>Alberta</u> is the oil capital of the <u>country</u>. Other oil rich areas of the world include the Middle East, Mexico, and northern Europe. The <u>amount</u> we use each year is in the <u>millions</u> of barrels.

Unfortunately, our <u>continent</u>, once <u>famous</u> for its rich oil wells, is running out of supplies. For this <u>reason</u>, the search for <u>possible</u> new wells is very important. The oil prospectors look for an <u>area</u> where they know certain rock formations lie

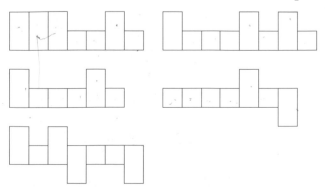

<u>beneath</u> the surface. With their electronic equipment, they can almost 'photograph' underground oil reserves using seismological waves. Through this method, oil has been discovered in the Arctic and under the sea near Newfoundland and Nova Scotia.

Observing Patterns

1. Find the list words that fit these shapes and write them in your notebook. Note that some of the words have capital letters.

2. Write the list words that answer these riddles.

a) Which word has two /f/ sounds but no letter **f**?

b) Which three words have two or four vowel letters, excluding **y**, but not three?

c) Which word has four syllables?

d) Which two words have double consonants?

e) Which two words have two syllables with stress on the second syllable?

f) Which word means almost the same as **well known**?

g) Which two words are found in the dictionary between the words **ready** / **tar sands**?

Discovering Patterns

photograph possible famous Calgary Manitoba station amount oil beneath area Canada reason Alberta continent millions country

1. Write the following list words:

       famous   **reason**   **amount**   **Canada**

Place a mark (´) over the stressed syllable. Say each of the words, listening for the vowel sound in the unstressed syllable. For example, in the word **famous**, we can't tell from the sound if it is spelled 'fam**u**s,' 'fam**i**s,' or 'fam**a**s'. We call this unstressed vowel a schwa /ə/, and we must find a way to remember how to spell it, besides the sound.

famus?   famis?

famas?   famous?

2. Write the four list words that are spelled with capital letters. What do these words have in common?

POWERBOOSTER

- The spelling of words with the schwa sound /ə/ must be studied carefully as there are many ways of spelling /ə/.

Exploring Patterns

1. It sometimes helps you remember the spelling of a schwa sound if you know a rhyming word that follows the same spelling pattern. Find the list word that rhymes with each of the following words, then write both words in your notebook.

billions   season   nation

2. Supply the correct letter or letters to spell the schwa in each of these words.

fam _ _ s	poss _ ble	phot _ graph	_ mount
cont _ n _ nt	Man _ tob _	Calg _ ry	Can _ d _

3. Complete each set of comparisons with a list word.
   a) **Calgary** is to **Alberta** as **Winnipeg** is to _____ .
   b) **Mayor** is to **city** as **prime minister** is to _____ .
   c) **Inside** is to **outside** as **above** is to _____ .

4. The words below are all related in meaning.

photograph	photography
photographic	photographer

Complete each sentence with one of the words above, then write the sentence.
   a) The _____ took a picture of the famous actor.
   b) I would like to study _____ at college.
   c) People who remember every detail of an event are said to have a _____ memory.
   d) I remember when that _____ was taken.

5. Look at each set, then write a word of your own that belongs to that set.
   a) Calgary   Yellowknife   _____
   b) Manitoba   Prince Edward Island   _____
   c) Canada   India   _____

6. There are many jobs in Canada that are exciting and done outdoors, such as working on an oil exploration crew. Other occupations are safer and quieter. Choose an occupation that you would like to try someday. Write a few sentences explaining why you think you would like this job, and why it's suited to you. Use some of these list words if you can.

reason   famous   Canada   possible   area

Be sure to proofread your sentences before you share them with a partner. Did your partner choose the same kind of occupation as you?

Challenges with Words

1. Read the paragraph and decide which Super Words to use in the blanks, then write out the words in your notebook.

The thick layers of _____ on the ocean floor can hide _____ reserves of oil. The _____ industry now uses _____ drilling rigs to search for these reserves. Modern oil _____ and high _____ water injection techniques can remove hundreds of barrels of oil a day.

◢◣◢◣◢◣◢◣◢◣━━━━━**WORDS IN HISTORY**━━━◢◣◢◣◢◣

In the 17th century in London, the surname of a famous hangman, <u>Derrick</u>, was used to name the gallows on which criminals were hanged. The tower of an oil drilling rig is called a **derrick** because originally it looked much like a gallows.

2. What's in a name? Write a girl's or boy's name that goes with these meanings.
   a) a list of what someone owes in a store or restaurant
   b) a flower from a thorny bush
   c) used to lift a car
   d) a month of the year

**sediment
petroleum
abundant
offshore
pressure
derricks**

3. Find the missing letters which make the schwa sound /ə/. Then write the complete words and mark the stressed syllable in each word with an accent. You may need to use your dictionary for help.

a) This is <u>another</u> new method.
b) <u>Carbon</u> is an element found in oil.
c) Methods of oil <u>recovery</u> have changed.
d) A <u>significant</u> new well was drilled last year.
e) It is important to <u>control</u> the flow of oil from a well.

4. **Offshore** is a compound word (**off** + **shore**) meaning 'moving or located far from shore'. Use **off** and the words on the oil barrel to make compound words that will fit these sentences.

a) The dog's off _____ all grew up to become champions.
b) The referee stopped play because our forward was off

_____ .

c) That was a very off _____ and unusual movie.
d) "Off _____ ," she said without thinking, "I'd say you're right."

5. **Word Exploration** There are twenty-two small words within the six Super Words in the unit. Can you find them without rearranging any of the letters? Three of the words are boys' names. One means 'to make a mistake', and one is a word for gasoline.

sediment   petroleum   abundant

offshore   pressure   derrick

6. The new words all have to do with the environment. Write the words that match the clues.

a) something you put on your skin to protect it from sun damage
b) rain that has been polluted by chemicals released into the air
c) material that can damage the health of living things

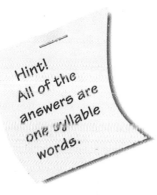

side
white
spring
hand

Hint!
All of the answers are one syllable words.

NEW WORDS

hazardous waste

sunblock

acid rain

STUDY STEPS

LOOK
SAY
COVER
WRITE
CHECK

Here is a list of words that may have been hard for you in Units 13–1
You and your teacher may add other words to the list.

known	matches	science	dangerous
furniture	objects	special	geography
picture	knives	treasures	possible
addresses	mountain	beginning	millions

1. Use the Study Steps for each word. Your teacher will dictate the words.

2. Complete the paragraph with words from the Study List. If you are correct, the circled letters will answer this riddle.

> What kind of bow is impossible to tie?
>
> a _____.

Dogs on the Job

It takes training and skill to be a police or resource dog, sniffing out _ _ _ _ _⊙_ _ _ criminals, or rescuing lost children. These dogs receive hours of _ _ _ _ _⊙_ training. They learn to search through thick bush, in high _ _ _ _ _ _⊙_ areas or cities where _ _ _ _ _ _⊙_ of people live. Sometimes they ha to find people or lost _⊙_ _ _ _ _ in small places where it is only _⊙_ _ _ _ _ _ _ for a dog to fit. Rescue dogs have been _ _ _⊙_ to save people trapped by earthquakes, in fires, or lost in the woods.

3. Supply the missing letter or letters for each of the words from the Study List. Write the words.

begi _ _ ing	tr _ _ s_ _ _
_ _ien _ _	_ _ives
pi _ t _ _ _	o _ je _ ts
f _ r _ _ t _ _ _	_ _ own
dang _ r _ _ _	g _ _ gr _ _ _y
m _ _nt _ _n	a _ _re _ _es

84

4. Select the correct word to complete each sentence. Use the number of syllables or the placement of stress to help you select the word.

    a) I found a (<u>3 syllables</u>) in the old trunk.

        picture   photograph   knife

    b) We ordered (<u>stress on 1st syllable</u>) at the restaurant.

        berries   spaghetti   dessert

    c) Science is helping to find answers for the problem of (<u>3 syllables, stress on 2nd syllable</u>).

        disease   <u>poverty</u>   pollution

5. Write the plural form of each picture word.

6. Find at least five words to add to each pattern for spelling the long **o** sound /ō/ as in **go**. You may use words from earlier units, your personal word list, classroom themes, or other subjects.

/ō/ spelled **oa** as in **coat**	/ō/ spelled **o** as in **cold**	/ō/ spelled **o_e** as in **rope**	/ō/ spelled **ow** as in **grow**

1. **Pronunciation Key:** Each entry word in a dictionary is followed by a pronunciation guide in brackets. When you understand the symbols, you will be able to pronounce a word even if you have never heard it before.

Example: escapade (eś kə pād)

    a) Study the pronunciation key below. Notice that each symbol is followed by a key word that tells you the sound.

a	hat	i	it	p	paper	v	very
ā	age	ī	ice	r	run	w	will
ä	far	j	jam	s	say	y	yet
b	bad	k	kind	sh	she	z	zero
ch	child	l	land	t	tel	zh	measure
d	did	m	me	TH	then		
e	let	n	no	th	thin	ə	represents
ē	be	ng	long	u	cup		the sound:
ėr	term	o	hot	u̇	ful	**a**	in above
f	fat	ö	go	ü	rule	**e**	in taken
g	go	ô	order			**i**	in pencil
h	he	oi	oil			**o**	in lemon
		ou	out			**u**	in circus

    b) Use the pronunciation key to match the pronunciations with these words from Units 13–17.

        (nīvz)   (griz´lēz)   (slō´lē)   (bōnz)

2. **Schwa:** The symbol /ə/ stands for the schwa sound. Find the schwa symbol in the pronunciation key. Notice that any vowel letter can make this sound. It is found only in unstressed syllables. For example, in the word **pencil**, the **i** makes the schwa sound.

    Write the words from Units 13–17 that match these pronunciations. Be careful to spell the schwa sound correctly.

        (fō´tə graf´)   (fer´nə chər)   (fa´məs)   (kon´tə nənt)

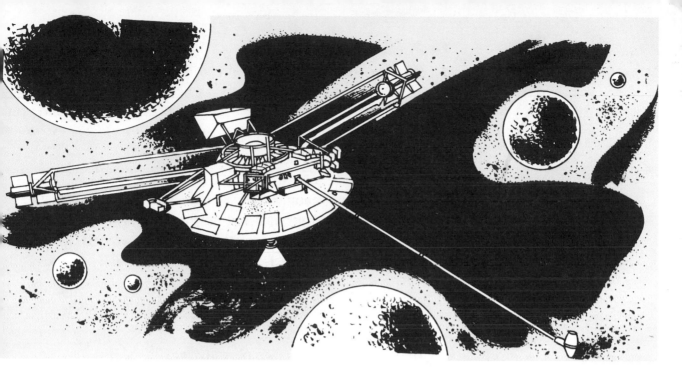

Exploring Space

1. On a clear night the sky is filled with countless twinkling objects. Write a list of all the objects, natural and invented, you might find in outer space. Classify them in a chart like this:

Planets	Stars	Satellites	Comets	Other
Earth	sun	Anik 1	Halley's	?

2. Some people believe there are intelligent life forms in the universe. What do you think two visitors from outer space would think of our planet? Write a conversation between two aliens who are visiting Earth.

Use this format:

First Alien: _____
Second Alien: _____

3. When you proofread your dialogue, use a dictionary to help you check the spelling of words you're not sure of.

Grammar Power

1. Writing with Adverbs: An adverb 'describes a verb'. A word is an adverb if it answers the questions when, where, or how an action took place.

When? *The news arrived finally. We hoped it would come sooner.*
Where? *Bring it here, don't leave it there.*
How? *The hippo swam slowly and lazily down the river.*

> **a)** Choose adverbs from the list below to complete the paragraph. All of the adverbs are from Units 1–18.

**especially   finally   suddenly   greatly   swiftly   silently
quietly   gracefully   lazily   slowly   usually   carefully**

_____ the door burst open. The girl came _____ and _____ into the room. She _____ placed the old box on the table and opened it _____ .

> **b)** Compare your paragraph with a partner's. How did the adverbs, each of you use, change the meaning of the paragraph?

2. Making Comparisons with Adverbs: You can make comparisons between two persons or things using adverbs just as you can with adjectives. If the adverb is short, like **fast** add **-er**. If it is long or ends in **-ly**, like **gracefully**, add **more** before the adverb.

Example: *A crocodile swims **faster** than a hippo.*
              *A seagull flies **more gracefully** than a turkey.*

Use your own ideas to complete these comparisons.
> **a)** An eagle flies **more swiftly** than _____ .
> **b)** A car travels **more quietly** than _____ .
> **c)** A train travels **more slowly** than _____ .

3. Joining Short Sentences: Many times when you are writing you may want to join two short sentences so they read more smoothly. combine them with **and** or **but**. When we do this, we use a comma before **and** or **but**.

Example: *I pulled the cord. The bus stopped.*
              I pulled the cord, and the bus stopped.

Use **and** or **but** to join the sentences below.

> **a)** I jumped in the puddle. My shoes got wet.
> **b)** My brother threw a water balloon. He missed me.
> **c)** Lisa made popcorn. We watched movies.
> **d)** Mr. Saliki asked a question. Nobody knew the answer.

Watch for changes in spelling, when -ly is added to words.
final — finally
lazy — lazily

Don't forget the commas!

Proofing Power

1. A spell check is a way to check the spelling of words typed into a computer. It is a program that checks for spelling mistakes and corrects them. Is a spell check the only answer for proofreading? Read the following poem and decide. Then correct any homophone errors you find.

O buoy, I have a spell cheque,
The best theirs ever bean.
I really don't know how two spell,
I just use my machine.
Let's run this poem threw it,
too sea if it is write...
Hay look! Knot even won mistake,
I'm glad that its so bright.

2. Read the following paragraph and write the words that are misspelled, giving their correct spelling.

I would love to go on a dangerus journey, wouldn't you? We could go into space and have a whole space mountian to ourselves. We could have furnature and a pitcher of our family on the wall. In our kitchen would be knifes, forks, and spoons. There might even be tresures in the peak of our mountain, or tiny objets to play with.

In the begining we might be lonely, but at least we could study geografy and sciense in an interesting place. Maybe it would be possable to invite our familes and friends. The trip would cost milions, but it's worth dreaming about.

19 Homophones Schwa Vowels

main mane plains planes
describe

plains

describe

microscope

receive

flower

hair

without

weather

stalk

main

passed

bean

scene

cells

pause

oxygen

Exploring the World of Grasses

We sit on it, play ball on it, and chew on it. Before the summer has <u>passed</u> we will cut it many times. Grasses are some of the commonest plants in the world. But we seldom <u>pause</u> to think of all the gifts we <u>receive</u> from these remarkable plants. How could we <u>describe</u> a summer <u>scene</u> <u>without</u> mentioning a soft carpet of fresh green grass under our feet? Grass gives off <u>oxygen</u> that we need to breathe. Wheat, the <u>main</u> grass crop on the western <u>plains</u>, gives us breakfast cereal and bread. Prairie grasses have roots that may be six metres deep. Each tiny root <u>hair</u> collects moisture from deep in the soil so the plant can survive dry <u>weather</u>. In high winds, the <u>stalk</u> of grass plants bends but doesn't break. Under the <u>microscope</u> we can see special <u>cells</u> in the stalk. These cells even straighten the grass plant if it is trampled to keep the seed and <u>flower</u> away from the soil. Like the <u>bean</u> plant, grasses such as wheat, rice, and oats are an excellent source of protein for animals and humans.

Observing Patterns

1. Write the list words that have the same spelling pattern and rhyme with the words below.

> chair mean gain bells feather cause walk

2. Write the list word that spells the sound /s/ with the same letters as in **scientist**.

3. **a)** Write the five list words that have two syllables.
    b) Write the two list words that have three syllables.

4. Write the three list <u>words</u> that would be found on a dictionary page with these guide words.

> parcel / plastic

Discovering Patterns

plains describe microscope receive flower
hair without weather stalk main
passed bean scene cells pause oxygen

1. Find a list word that sounds the same as each of these words in the puzzles but has a different meaning and spelling. Write the pairs in your notebook.

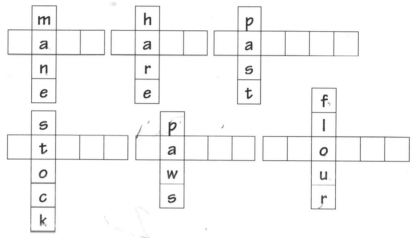

2. Write the following list words and place an accent over the syllable that is stressed.

receive   describe   microscope   oxygen

Now say the words aloud, listening for the schwa sounds in the unstressed syllables. Circle the letter or letters that spell the schwa sound.

POWERBOOSTER

- Words that sound the same but have different meanings and sometimes spellings are called **homophones**.
- Most vowels in unstressed syllables make the schwa sound / ə/. Pay special attention when learning to spell such words.

Exploring Patterns

1. Select the correct homophones from the word box to write the sentences.

plains	planes	flower	flour	scene	seen
cell	sell	hair	hare	stalk	stock
bean	been	main	mane	past	passed

a) We looked at the beautiful winter _____ from the window.
b) Do you _____ any _____ seeds here?
c) I _____ by a lovely _____ bed at the _____ entrance to the school.
d) The young _____ munched on a _____ of celery.
e) Have you ever _____ so many _____ in the air?

2. Complete the list words on each plant.

p _ _ s _ _   w _ _ ther   ox _ g _ n   _ _ en _
st _ _ k   rec _ _ ve   d _ s _ _ ibe

3. The words **microscope** and **telescope** come from Greek. Read these word meanings and use them to write a definition for the above two words. The definitions are started for you.

scope—scientific instrument for helping the eye or ear to make observations
micro—small
tele—far off

a) A microscope is an instrument used to help the eye see things that are _____ .
b) A telescope is an instrument used to help the eye see things that are _____ .

4. Draw word webs for two of the following list words.

hair   weather   flower   microscope

Example:

```
                                              sprout
                              earth  →   roots
giant  ←        bean
                          →   vegetable
     beanstalk        soup                   garden
golden egg   harp   bread   butter   carrots        peas
```

5. Before you stretches a beautiful field of soft green grass. List five words that describe the way the grass looks and feels. Then list five words that describe what you like to play or do on grass.

6. Using the word lists you made in exercise 5, write a short paragraph about what you would do if you were the kids in the picture. Be sure to proofread your paragraph for spelling errors with a partner.

Challenges with Words

1. Circle the word which doesn't belong in each set of words, and explain why it doesn't belong.

Example:

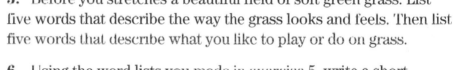

    a) lake, slough, (grass), river, creek, pond

Grass is not a body of water.

b) wheat, leaves, rye, barley, oats, rice
c) field, elevator, prairie, lowland, tundra
d) Saskatchewan, Prince Albert, Brandon, St. John, Regina
e) buffalo, polar bear, pronghorn, coyote, jack-rabbit
f) hawk, eagle, duck, snake, crow

whether
prairie
Saskatchewan
slough
pollen
wheat

2. Match the Canadian place names on the suitcase with their word origins.

    a) named for Queen Victoria's husband, Albert
    b) comes from a Cree word meaning 'murky water'
    c) means 'New Scotland'
    d) named after the captain who discovered it
    e) named for the wife of King George III
    f) named after the Outaouais people

3. Homophone hunt! There are 36 words in the puzzle below. Each of the words is a homophone. Start at any letter and move in any direction, but don't skip over letters.

Example: serial

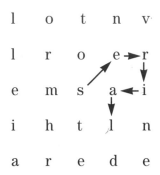

```
l   o   t   n   v
l   r   o   e → r
e   m   s   a ← i
i   h   t   l   n
a   r   e   d   e
```

Now write the homophones for the words you have found.
Example: serial—cereal

Homophones are words that sound the same but have different spellings and meanings.

4. Use the letters of the word **Saskatchewan** to write as many smaller words as you can. Score one point for each word.

5. Choose three Super Words. For each one, write nine words which have something to do with the Super Word. Arrange your words into a triangle poem as in the example below.

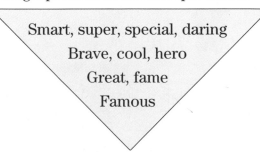
Smart, super, special, daring
Brave, cool, hero
Great, fame
Famous

6. Write the food words that fit the sentences below.
    a) A _____ makes a great pocket sandwich.
    b) _____ is made from soya beans.
    c) A _____ is made from thinly sliced meat.

NEW WORDS

gyros

tofu

pita

20

-ed Ending
excit**ed** grabb**ed**

excited
watched
captain
believed
mapped
officer
grabbed
stepped
Vancouver
remembered
village
arrived
British
attacked
dropped
toward

Exploring the Routes to Canada

Immigrants have been coming to Canada's west coast for more than 12 000 years! It is <u>believed</u> that the first Canadians <u>arrived</u> on foot. They crossed a land bridge from Asia and began to spread out <u>toward</u> the south and east. Two hundred years ago, <u>British</u> and Spanish newcomers arrived in ships to fight over who would control this land. They <u>grabbed</u> whole islands, <u>attacked</u> each other's settlements, and ignored the fact that the native people had been there for thousands of years.
One young <u>officer,</u> who had joined the British navy when he was only thirteen, sailed around the world with the explorer, <u>Captain</u> Cook. His name was George, and he <u>mapped</u> much of the Pacific west coast. He is <u>remembered</u> because he left his name, <u>Vancouver</u>, on the island and the city where his ship <u>dropped</u> anchor and he <u>stepped</u> ashore. It would have <u>excited</u> early Canadians to have <u>watched</u> how the small <u>village</u> of Vancouver turned into the beautiful city it is today.

Observing Patterns

1. Write the two list words that begin with a capital letter.

2. Write the eight list words that have double consonants. Then circle the double consonants in each word.

3. Find the correct letter or letters for the schwa sound in these list words, then write the words.

capt _ _ n   off _ cer   t _ ward

_ rrived   _ ttacked

93

4. Complete each sentence with list words.

   a) The children were very _____ as they _____ the circus.

   b) Andrew _____ that the money was in the attic but nobody _____ him.

Discovering Patterns

excited watched captain believed mapped officer grabbed stepped Vancouver remembered village arrived British attacked dropped toward

1. Write the list words below that have the ending **-ed**, and underline the base word in each. Notice what happens to the base word when the ending **-ed** is added.

watched	mapped	grabbed	stepped	believed
remembered	arrived	excited	attacked	dropped

2. Sort the words from exercise 1 into the chart below.

Final Consonant Doubled	Final e Dropped	No change to Base Word
mapped	arrived	watched

3. Examine the words that double final consonants. What is similar about their base words? Try to state a rule for adding **-ed** to base words like this.

4. Examine the words that drop an **e**. What is similar about their base words? Try to state a rule for adding **-ed** to base words like this.

POWERBOOSTER

- When adding **-ed** to single syllable words ending in vowel-consonant, double the consonant, as in grab — gra**bb**ed.
- When adding **-ed** to base words ending in silent **e**, drop the **e**, as in excite — excit**ed**.

Exploring Patterns

1. Add **-ed** to each base word below. Remember, some base words change when **-ed** is added.

> battle   laugh   shop   capture   slip   bump

2. The /ch/ sound is sometimes spelled with the consonants **tch** as in **watched**. Combine the letters on the word wheel to spell as many words as you can with the **tch** pattern.

Example:

> $m + a + tch + ed$
> $= matched$

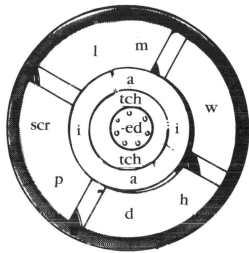

3. Combine each pair of short sentences into a longer sentence.

a) The captain dropped the ship's anchor. Then he stepped into the rowboat.

b) The British officers attacked the fort. They believed the enemy was hiding inside.

c) The village people watched the parade. They were very excited.

4. Complete each analogy with a list word.

a) **Miserable** is to **happy** as **bored** is to _____ .

b) **Airplane** is to **pilot** as **ship** is to _____ .

c) **Doubted** is to **believed** as **forgotten** is to _____ .

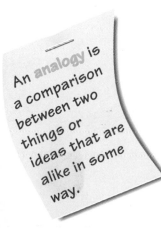

An **analogy** is a comparison between two things or ideas that are alike in some way.

5. Sequence is important when you are writing about action. The reader wants to know what happened first, second, third, and so on. Work with a partner. Each of you outline the events of something exciting that has happened to you.

Have your partner check the sequence before you write it in paragraph form. Is the order clear? You may want to use some of these list words in your paragraph.

excited   grabbed   watched   attacked

Challenges with Words

1. Use the correct Super Words in the paragraph about Captain Cook.

After the age of 24, Cook was rarely _____ from the sea he loved. When he was _____ to lieutenant, he _____ the ship Endeavour. On his many voyages he took _____ of all lands he visited, in the name of the king. His adventures were ended, however, on a Pacific Island. There, in a _____ over the _____ of a boat, he died at the age of 51.

2. The letters **-ed**, when used at the end of a word, make three sounds: /əd/, /t/, and /d/. Make a chart like the one below in your notebook.

/əd/	/t/	/d/
separated promoted	placed	saved

Write other **-ed** words that fit the chart. Here are a few to get you started.

forced   judged   waited   scrubbed   seated

SUPER WORDS

commanded
promoted
possession
theft
skirmish
separated

96

Hint!
One of the answers is a Super Word.

3. Add the suffix **-ion** to the words in the box to complete the sentences.

a) The police got a _____ from the thief.

b) We planted trees for _____ from the wind.

c) She was sad to lose the only _____ she ever liked.

d) "Can you give me _____s to City Hall?"

e) The static electricity in the science show _____ made our hair stand on end.

| possess |
| protect |
| direct |
| demonstrate |
| confess |

4. Look up **skirmish** in your dictionary and write its meaning. Five synonyms are used in the following sentences. Unscramble the letters and write the words.

a) The **l a r q r e u** turned into a **e s f c l u f** before the police arrived.

b) The customer had a heated **m u t a g n r e** with the manager.

c) No **e a l t b t** or military **h a l c s** had ever started so quickly.

5. A sea map or chart was made by explorers whenever they discovered new territory. Make a chart of some place you know or have explored — an apartment complex, a neighbourhood creek, or a shopping mall. Label your chart 'area of discovery' with information strangers would need to find their way around. Give colourful names to interesting features on your map.

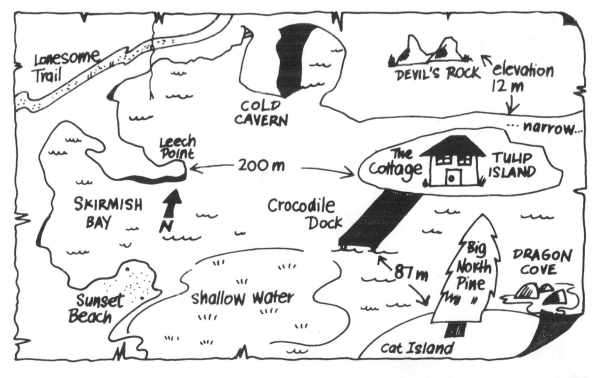

21

-ed -ing Endings

dried   dreaming   hiding

pioneer
buried
carried
married
replied
dried
coming
dreaming
having
hiding
missing
husband
teachers
doctors
log
chimney

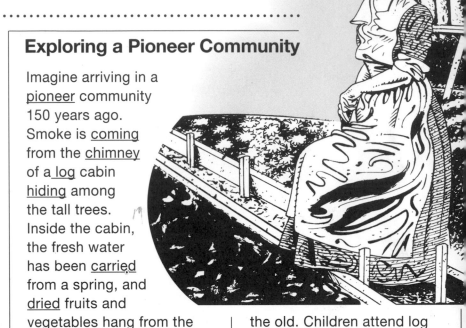

Exploring a Pioneer Community

Imagine arriving in a pioneer community 150 years ago. Smoke is coming from the chimney of a log cabin hiding among the tall trees. Inside the cabin, the fresh water has been carried from a spring, and dried fruits and vegetables hang from the ceiling. The pioneer husband and wife may be missing some of the comforts they left behind, but they are having an exciting time building a new life. They can't waste time dreaming of the old. Children attend log schools where teachers have eight grades in one room. There are no hospitals or doctors nearby, but there may be a simple church where people are married and buried.

Observing Patterns

1. Write the list word that completes each statement.
   a) We are students and they are _____ .
   b) She is a wife and he is a _____ .
   c) You are patients and they are _____ .

2. Write two sets of list words that rhyme with each other. One set has three rhyming words and the other has two.

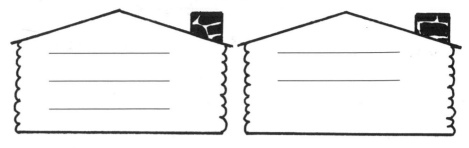

3. Write the nine list words that would come between **chalk** and **lucky** in the dictionary.

4. Write the list words that have double vowels or consonants.

Discovering Patterns

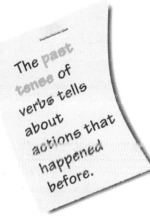

The *past tense* of verbs tells about actions that happened before.

pioneer buried carried married replied dried coming dreaming having hiding missing husband teachers doctors log chimney

1. **a)** What do the final two letters in these verbs have in common?

bury reply carry marry dry

b) Write the list words that spell the past tense of the verbs above.

c) What happens to the base word when -**ed** is added to the verbs in a)?

2. **a)** What do the final two letters of these verbs have in common?

come have hide

b) Write the list words that are related to the verbs above.

c) What happens to the base word when -**ing** is added to the verbs in a)?

POWERBOOSTER

- When adding -**ed** to verbs ending in a consonant + **y**, change the **y** to **i** and add -**ed**, as in **buried**.
- When adding -**ing** to verbs ending in a consonant + **e**, drop the **e** and add -**ing**, as in **hiding**.

1. Add **-ed** or **-ing** to the base words on the log cabin.

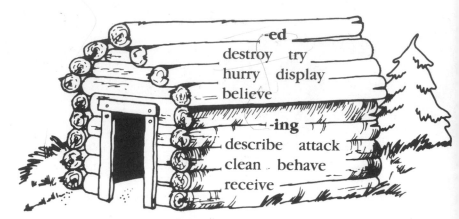

-ed
destroy   try
hurry   display
believe

-ing
describe   attack
clean   behave
receive

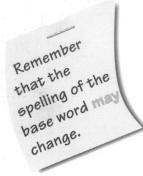

Remember that the spelling of the base word may change.

2. Write a list word to replace each underlined word below.
<u>Early</u> life in Canada was not easy. A wife and her <u>spouse</u> usually <u>brought</u> little money or supplies with them. They found that <u>educators</u> and <u>physicians</u> were <u>lacking</u> in the new land. The settlers were often not ready for the <u>arrival</u> of the cold winter. Before long, however, they built <u>wooden</u> cabins and started <u>hoping</u> once again that life in the new land would be happy.

3. Many of the list words contain the long **e** sound as in **feet**. Write the list words that spell /ē/ the same as in each of these words.

meat   freedom   donkey   hurried

4. The word **pioneer** comes from the French word <u>pionnier</u>, which meant 'a soldier who goes ahead of an army to prepare the route'. Write a sentence to explain how each of the following people could be called a **pioneer**.
   a) an early Canadian settler
   b) a modern astronaut
   c) a medical researcher

Can you think of other kinds of pioneers?

5. What would pioneer children say if they could see the cities that stand where their first log or sod houses stood? Write a paragraph describing what you imagine your community looked like when it was first settled. Use some of these list words in your paragraph.

missing   **coming**   **log**   **pioneer**

Challenges with Words

1. Write the Super Words that fit the blanks in these sentences.
a) **Colonist** is to **colony** as **settler** is to _____ .
b) **Civilized** is to **city** as **wild** is to _____ .
c) **Wax** is to **spread** as **paint** is to _____ .
d) **Followed** is to **obeyed** as **provided** is to _____ .
e) **Barns** are to **animals** as **log houses** are to _____ .
f) **Prisoner** is to **pardoned** as **slave** is to _____ .

frontier ✓
applied
colonists
settlement ✓
supplied ✓
freed ✓

━━━ ━━━ ━━━◢ **WORDS IN HISTORY** ◣━━━ ━━━ ━━━

> The word **settle** comes from the Anglo-Saxon word <u>setl</u>, 'a seat', and from <u>setlan</u>, 'to place something in a seat'.

2. Add **-ed** or **-ing** to the words in brackets. Use your dictionary if you're not sure of the correct spelling.

Many farmers (settle) on the thickly (wood) areas along the Saint Lawrence River. For them, (create) a home in the wilderness was difficult. After (arrive) in early spring, they first had to clear the land. This job was hard, and often the settlers (rely) on their neighbours for help. Children too (scurry) about, (run) errands and (lend) a hand. (Dig) the soil for crops and (choose) the right logs for a home were important tasks to do the first year the pioneers (settle) on the new land.

3. The colonists who settled in Canada came from many countries. Today people are still settling here. Write a paragraph explaining how your family or someone you know came to settle here.

4. What was it like in the pioneer days of your community? Make up the first page of a newspaper which might have been published back then. You can use a history book, an encyclopedia, or a CD-ROM on a computer to find facts about pioneer life. Use as many of the Super Words as you can in your pioneer newspaper.

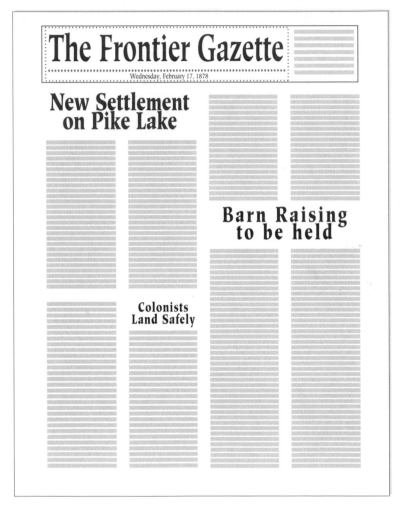

The Frontier Gazette
Wednesday, February 17, 1878

New Settlement on Pike Lake

Barn Raising to be held

Colonists Land Safely

5. These new words are all old words with new meanings. Unscramble the words that fit each meaning. Notice what happens when **-ed** is added to **scan** and **log**.

    a) He **lscodelr** down the text to proofread his story.

    b) Anna **no gdogel** to the computer and called up her file.

    c) We **dnncsae** photographs with our computer scanner, so we could illustrate our story.

NEW WORDS

scanned

scrolled

logged on

Number Words

forty   twice

volleyball
score
twice
Olympic
court
sport
trophy
hands
player
eleven
forty
points
guard
shoot
twenty-five
eighteen

Exploring the Sport of Volleyball

Did you know?
• Volleyball has been an Olympic sport since 1964.
• A game of volleyball is won by the first team to score fifteen points, but they must win by a margin of two. Therefore, a winning score may be as high as twenty-five or even more.
• A volleyball court is eighteen metres long and nine metres wide.
• A player may not touch the ball twice in a row.
• A volleyball player can hit the ball with the hands or upper body.
• Players must guard against touching the net. It's a foul if they do.
• The server must shoot the ball inside the court boundaries.
• More than 150 countries, including Canada, compete for a trophy in international volleyball competition.
• Volleyball is popular with all ages, from eleven to forty.

Observing Patterns

1. Write the list words that answer these riddles.
    a) I am the end parts of your arms and I am part of a clock.
    b) I am the record of points in a game and I rhyme with **more**.
    c) I am two times and I rhyme with **mice**.

2. Write the list words that have two syllables and list words that have three syllables.

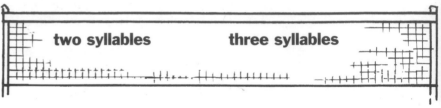

two syllables   **three syllables**

3. Write the list words that fit these shapes.

Discovering Patterns

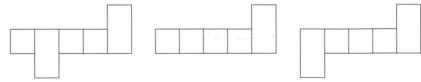

volleyball score twice Olympic court sport trophy hands player eleven forty points guard shoot twenty-five eighteen

1. Write the number word for 18. Now write the number word that 18 comes from. What happens to the base word when **-teen** is added?

2. Write the number word for 40. Now write the number word that 40 comes from. What happens to the base word when **-ty** is added?

3. Write the number word for 25. What happens when a single digit (such as 5) is added to a number word such as **twenty**?

4. Write the number that the word **twice** comes from.

POWERBOOSTER

- Number words are often based on related numbers as with **eighteen** and **eight**. It is important to notice when a letter has been changed from one number to another, as with **four** and **forty**.

Exploring Patterns

1. Write the following mathematics questions as number words. Also write the answers in words.

    a) 18 + 25 − 3 = _____

    b) 11 + 17 + 21 = _____

    c) 45 − 18 − 16 = _____

2. The list word **court** has many dictionary definitions. Write the number of the definition that fits each sentence below.

> **court** (kôrt) **1** a royal palace **2** a space partly or wholly enclosed by walls or buildings **3** a place marked off for games **4** a place where justice is carried out **5** try to gain the love of; seek to marry

    a) The team practised on the new basketball court.

    b) After the ceremony the queen returned to the court.

    c) In fairy tales the prince usually courts the princess.

    d) The children played safely on the quiet court.

    e) The criminal was sentenced in court.

3. Complete the list words on the volleyballs.

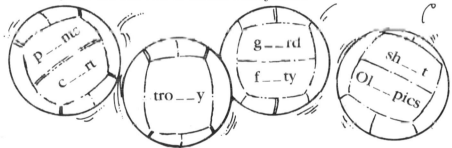

4. A spelling chart in a dictionary could help you to locate and spell many of the list words. Carefully examine the partial spelling chart below. Match a key word in the chart which would help you to spell **trophy**, **guard**, or **eighteen**.

Sound	Beginnings of Words	Middles of Words	Ends of Words
g	go, ghost guess	bogus, boggle exact	bag, egg rogue
ā	age, aid eight, eh	face, fail straight payment, vein, break	say, weigh, they
f	fat, phone	heifer, coffee, laughter, gopher	

5. What's your favourite game or sport? In a few sentences, explain why you like it so much. You may want to use some of these list words.

sport   **score**   **player**   **shoot**

Start your sports story something like this:

> My favourite sport is _____ .
> I enjoy it because _____ .

Have a partner proofread your writing for spelling and punctuation errors. You proofread your partner's. How do errors affect your enjoyment or understanding of the writing?

Challenges with Words

1. Use the correct Super Word to complete each of the following sentences below.

   a) In football the team which is playing _____ has control of the ball.
   b) A soccer field is about _____ metres long.
   c) Every sport has a different style of _____ .
   d) The ninth is usually the last _____ in a baseball game.
   e) Basketball is often played in a _____ .
   f) A softball _____ throws the ball underhand.

inning
uniform
gymnasium
pitcher
offence
ninety-nine

2. Number words, such as **ninety-nine**, are used when writing bank cheques. Using the sample bank cheque as a model, write cheques of your own for the amounts listed below.

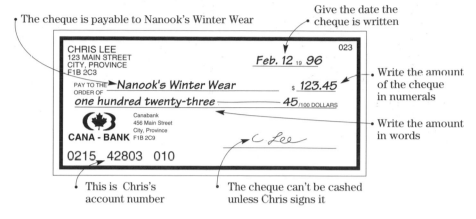

The cheque is payable to Nanook's Winter Wear

Give the date the cheque is written

Write the amount of the cheque in numerals

Write the amount in words

This is Chris's account number

The cheque can't be cashed unless Chris signs it

a) Pay to: Sports Unlimited; for $35.26

b) Pay to: (your town) Midget Hockey League; for $23.48

c) Pay to: Bruno's Pizzeria; for $11.92

d) Pay to: Town Hardware Ltd.; for $99.37

e) Pay to: (Your school); for $17.50

3. Sports have their own terms or vocabulary. Match up the term in Group A with the sport in Group B.

Group A.   spike, home run, blue line, sweep, free throw, love, slalom, first down, penalty kick.

Group B: hockey, football, volleyball, soccer, basketball, baseball, tennis, curling, skiing.

4. Choose a team sport you like to play and make a booklet describing how to play it. You might organize your booklet like this:

- Title page
- Table of contents
- A drawing of the playing field or court
- A list of the players on each team and how their position is played
- A description of how the game is played and the method of scoring
- A dictionary or glossary of common terms used in the sport

In football, the ball is sometimes called a pigskin, because the balls used to be made from pig leather.

23

Long e ie ea
Prefix un-

p**ie**ces app**ear** **un**usual

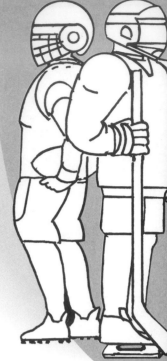

clothing

unfinished

suit

except

unusual

pair

appear

unpacked

loose

pieces

reaches

unidentified

size

pants

making

right

Exploring the World of Clothing

People have been wearing <u>clothing</u> for a long time. The first clothes were probably <u>loose</u>, <u>unfinished</u> <u>pieces</u> of fur. They kept the body warm and protected. We still wear clothes for protection, but we also wear them to tell other people who we are. Imagine two <u>unidentified</u> hockey teams trying to play a game. <u>Except</u> for the uniforms, how do we know which team scores? We also wear clothes to make ourselves look and feel good. Bright colours have a way of <u>making</u> us feel happy. Clothes that are the <u>right</u> <u>size</u> feel comfortable. Some people wear <u>unusual</u> clothes to <u>appear</u> different. A clown <u>reaches</u> for a <u>pair</u> of baggy <u>pants</u> or a <u>suit</u> that looks like it has just been <u>unpacked</u> from someone's pocket when he's trying to make us laugh. Above all, clothes still keep us warm and protected just as they did a million years ago.

Observing Patterns

1. Write the list words that fit the clues. Say the words out loud — some of them are tricky.

    a) I have 3 syllables and 10 letters. _ _ _ _ _ _ _ _ _ _

    b) I have 4 syllables and only 7 letters. _ _ _ _ _ _ _

    c) I have 5 syllables and 12 letters. _ _ _ _ _ _ _ _ _ _ _ _

2. Write the list words that are in the same word families as the following words. Remember, members of a word family rhyme and follow the same spelling pattern.

Example: tight — right

tight   goose   fruit   chair

peaches   fear   nieces   raking

3. Complete these sentences with list words.

I opened my suitcase and _____ my socks, shirts, and other pieces of _____ . I put everything away _____ an old shirt and a pair of _____ .

Discovering Patterns

*clothing unfinished suit except unusual
pair appear unpacked loose pieces right
reaches unidentified size pants making*

1. Write the list words that are related to these base words.

usual   finish   pack   identify

What does the prefix **un-** do to the meaning of each of the base words?

2. Write three list words that have the sound /ē/ as in **bee**. Underline the letters that spell the /ē/ sound.

POWERBOOSTER

- The prefix **un-** usually means 'not' and changes the meaning of a base word to its opposite.
- The sound /ē/ can be spelled **ie** as in **pieces** or **ea** as in **reaches**.

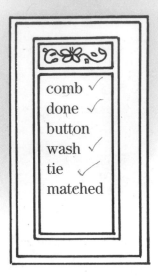

comb ✓
done ✓
button
wash ✓
tie ✓
matched

Exploring Patterns

1. The little girl is very untidy! Describe her by adding the prefix **un-** to words on the mirror.

Her face is _____ .

Her hair is _____ .

Her buttons are _____ .

Her shoelaces are _____ .

Her socks are _____ .

Her overalls are _____ .

2. The words below are built on the list words **except**, **appear**, and **suit**. Complete each sentence with one of the words. Underline the parts that were added.

> **exception   disappear   suitcase**
> **appearance   unsuitable**

a) The _____ of the house made us think that it was empty.

b) I'm sorry, but this shirt is _____ for the party.

c) We will make an _____ to the rule this time.

d) Don't forget your _____ at the airport.

e) How did you make the rabbit _____ ?

3. Make a word pole with the word **clothing**. Add one clothing word for each letter. The pole has been started for you.

```
C
L
O
B A T H I N G   S U I T
H
I
N
G
```

4. Why are these kids wearing special clothing? Write a sentence or two telling the purpose of each outfit.

5. What's the best outfit you've ever worn on a special occasion? Describe your favourite outfit using some of these list words.

pants   pair   size   unusual   pieces

Challenges with Words

1. Match the correct Super Word to each set of words below. Then add a word of your own to each set.

a) create   plan   _____
b) old-fashioned   unpopular   _____
c) valuable   costly   _____
d) look   expression   _____
e) equipment   supplies   _____
f) ugly   homely   _____

2. The prefix un- means 'not' or 'the opposite'.

a) Choose the correct word in the box to complete the newspaper article.

POLICE UN _____ MISSING JEANS

Today, police un _____ the true story of the missing designer jeans. It has been two months since their un _____ disappearance. Then a shipment of jeans with un _____ cuffs and an un _____ logo turned up in a downtown store. When a thread was pulled from one of the logos, it began to un _____ , revealing the famous symbol.

b) If you look in your dictionary under **un**-, you will see there are dozens of words which have this prefix. Choose five of them to write your own sentences.

appearance
expensive
materials
design
unattractive
unfashionable

even
ravel
usual
cover
familiar
folded

3. Add the suffix **-ance** to the words below and match them to the correct definition.

attend   clear   insure   resist   perform

a) room to spare around the edges

b) being present at a place

c) an opposing force

d) the giving of a play or other show

e) protection against risk

4. **Design** comes from the Latin word <u>signum</u>, which meant 'a mark or signal'. Use your dictionary to find as many words as you can which come from the same root as **signal**. Hint! try looking under prefixes such as **con-**, or **re-**.

5. Designers use a personal trademark or logo to identify their products, such as jeans, shirts, and even sunglasses. Some logos are animals, while others are formed from the initials of the designer. Design a personal logo for yourself. Then you can use it on book covers, art work, or just to identify things that belong to you.

spokesperson
supermodel
unisex

6. The new words come from the world of fashion and advertising. Write the words that fit the sentences.

a) If I'm designed for both males and females, I'm called

_____ .

b) If I'm famous around the world and I model designer clothes, I may be a _____ .

c) I can be male or female and I advertise a particular product. I'm a _____ .

STUDY STEPS

LOOK
SAY
COVER
WRITE
CHECK

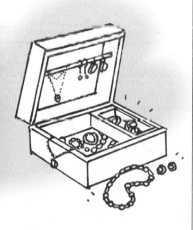

Remember to change some base words before adding -ed.

Here is a list of words that may have been hard for you in Units 19–23. You and your teacher may add other words to the list.

believed	stepped	flower	forty
excited	pieces	guard	unidentified
having	except	remembered	receive
without	coming	eighteen	scene

1. Use the Study Steps for each word. Your teacher will dictate the words.

2. Complete the story with words from the Study List. Write the story in your notebook.

It was a mystery how the _u_____ stranger got past the _g_____ and into the mansion. No one at the _s_____ of the crime had _r_____ seeing anything unusual _e_____ for a wilted yellow _f_____ that had been _s_____ on by the intruder. Some _p_____ of broken glass lay on the ground outside the window. The police _b_____ that the robber left _w_____ finding the jewels he had come for. An _e_____ crowd of thirty or _f_____ people watched the detectives _c_____ and going. They did not _r_____ any news, and soon they left for home.

3. Complete each study word.

rec _ _ve   f _ _ty   _ _ _ _teen   bel _ _ved
p _ _ces   _ _ _ept   g _ _rd   _ _ _ited
fl _ _ er   _ _ene   ste _ _ ed

4. Finish the chart by adding **-ed** to the base words.

Base Word	-ed
miss	
carry	
drop	
believe	
watch	
trap	
bury	
taste	

5. Use each word in the homophone pairs in a separate sentence to show that you understand its meaning.

   a) flower, flour
   b) bean, been
   c) seen, scene

6. Write the answer to each of these problems in number words.

   $7 + 8 + 12 - 9 =$ _____
   $13 + 24 + 6 - 3 =$ _____
   $43 - 7 - 19 + 8 =$ _____
   $18 - 3 + 12 - 16 =$ _____

7. Use each clue to find a letter. Then use the letters and code to find the answer to the riddle below.

   This letter is in **bean** but not in **been**.   1 _
   This letter is in **hair** but not in **hare**.   2 _
   This letter is in **sport** but not in **strap**.   3 _
   This letter is in **dried** but not in **rice**.   4 _
   This letter is in **loose** but not in **clone**.   5 _
   This letter is in **hiding** but not in **dressing**.   6 _
   This letter is in **stepped** but not in **shepherd**.   7 _
   This letter is in **weather** but not in **feather**.   8 _

Question: What is as big as a hippopotamus but **weighs** nothing?
Answer: $\overline{~}~\overline{~}~\overline{~}~~~\overline{~}~\overline{~}~\overline{~}~\overline{~}~\overline{~}~\overline{~}$
         2 7 5   5 6 1 4 3 8

I before E?
I before e
except after
c and when it
says ā as in
neighbour and
weigh.

Dictionary Skills

1. Idioms: The expression *get out of my hair* means 'go away and stop bothering me'. This expression is called an idiom. An idiom is a phrase or expression whose meaning cannot be understood from the meaning of its individual words.

Most idioms can be found in the dictionary by deciding which word in the expression is the most important. You will usually find the idiom listed at the end of the entry for that word.

Study the idioms listed below for **hand**.

Idioms	Meanings
have one's hands full	be very busy
lend a hand	help or assist
on the other hand	from the opposite point of view

Choose an idiom that fits each sentence below. Write the sentence.

   a) Would you please _____ lifting this box?

   b) My parents _____ with my baby sister.

   c) I want the bicycle very much; _____ , I can't afford it.

2. Try to rewrite each sentence below to show that you understand the idiom. Use your dictionary for help.

Example: **We're in hot water** *means 'We're in trouble'.*

   a) Please drop me a line.
   b) Gerry is a fair weather friend.
   c) Stop pulling my leg.
   d) We're all in the same boat.

Exploring the World of Sports

1. People enjoy playing many different kinds of sports. Make a chart of all the sports played by members of your group. For each sport, list the equipment used. For example:

Sport	Equipment
Volleyball	net ball
Ping pong	paddles ball

2. Choose a sport from your chart that you enjoy playing or watching. Write a paragraph describing how this sport is played. Be sure to explain how the equipment you have listed is used.

3. Check the spelling of the equipment in your dictionary. Have a friend read your description to make sure it is clear.

Grammar Power

1. Using Collective Nouns: Sometimes, nouns describe a whole collection of things or people: a **flock** of birds; a **herd** of cows. We call these special nouns **collective** nouns.

Write the collective noun from the box that fits each phrase below.

crowd
flock
herd
bunch
team
hive
school
pair

a _____ of shoes
a _____ of bees
a _____ of flowers
a _____ of pigeons
a _____ of deer
a _____ of fish
a _____ of ballplayers
a _____ of people

2. Make up your own collective nouns for these groups:
a) a _____ of umpires
b) a _____ of news photographers
c) a _____ of computer games
d) a _____ of jet skis.

3. Making Subject and Verb Agree: A collective noun, such as **class**, or **team**, is singular, even though it is made up of many members. When you use a collective noun, the verb must be singular too.

Example: **Whales swim** *past the boat.*
            but
            *A **pod** of whales **swims** past the boat.*

Write the correct form of the verb for each sentence below.
a) A new pair of shoes (costs, cost) a lot of money.
b) The herd of horses (gallops, gallop) across the field.
c) That bunch of flowers (smells, smell) great!
d) The flock of geese (flies, fly) south in winter.

Other collectives include: a pride of lions, a murder of crows, a smack of jellyfish.

4. Past, Present, or Future: Every sentence we write tells the reader when the action takes place. It could be in the past, present, or future.

present— I see   I am seeing   **past**— I saw   **future**— I will see

Write the verb in the correct tense in these sentences. Look for adverbs such as **today** or **yesterday**, to tell you if the action is in the past, present, or future.

    a) Someday people (*live, will live, lived*) in communities linked by computers.

    b) Already, some developers (*are planning, planned, will plan*) high-tech neighbourhoods.

    c) In the past, people (*visit, will visit, visited*) their neighbours, or (*talk, will talk, talked*) on the telephone.

    d) Now, they (*get together, will get together, got together*) by e-mail.

Proofing Power

Read the following paragraph carefully, with a partner. See how many mistakes you can spot. Often proofreaders work as a team.

I beleive that the most exciteing thing in the world is sports. I dreamd of having a career as a professional athlete. Their is just one thing— I'm no good at sports. This year I tryed soccer. When I remembered to were shin pads, I forgot to waer my game socks. When I seen the ball comeing, I steped forward and kickt it with all my might. Usually, it didn't move. But once, when I was playing gaurd, I actually scord—for the other team! My coach said that I wood receive a medal at the end of the season. I did. The "Most Effort" award!

25

Possessives

father's   cousin's

terrible
voice
painter's
father's
lizard
crooked
enough
noise
scary
spooky
editor's
drank
writer's
cousin's
laughing
though

Exploring the World of Stories and Pictures

Ever wonder how a <u>writer's</u> or <u>painter's</u> imagination works? <u>Though</u> you may not know it, an artist usually gets <u>enough</u> ideas just from observing ordinary life. A painter might get an idea for the illustration of a <u>spooky</u> old mansion from a neighbourhood house. A <u>lizard</u> in a pet store might be a model for a huge, <u>scary</u> dinosaur. A writer might get ideas for someone in a story from little details in the people she knows. A <u>father's</u> <u>crooked</u> smile, a <u>cousin's</u> <u>laughing</u> <u>voice</u>, or the <u>noise</u> a friend made as he <u>drank</u> through a straw could all give life to a story character. Of course, not all ideas are good —some are <u>terrible</u>! That's why it is the <u>editor's</u> job to make the pictures and words in a story work together. You can use your own experience to write and draw. Just listen to your friends and watch what they do. Good ideas are all around.

Observing Patterns

1. Write the two three-syllable list words.

2. Write the two list words in which **gh** spells the sound /f/ as in **funny**.

3. Write the nine two-syllable list words that have the stress on the first syllable.

4. Complete each set with a list word.
    a) bent   twisted   _____
    b) miserable   awful   _____
    c) honking   blaring   _____
    d) sipped   slurped   _____

117

5. Write the list words that would be found in the dictionary between **slippery** and **volcano**.

Discovering Patterns

terrible voice painter's father's lizard crooked enough noise scary spooky genie's drank writer's cousin's laughing though

1. Write the list words that end in an apostrophe and **s** ('s). These words mean 'belonging to...' and are called **possessives**. **Possessives** are formed by adding **'s** to a base word. Underline the base word in each possessive list word.

2. Complete each phrase with one of the possessive list words.

the _____ corrections

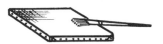

the _____ novel

the _____ canvas and brush

the _____ footprints

118

Exploring Patterns

1. Replace each underlined phrase in the following sentences with a possessive form. Write the sentence.

    a) The <u>toy belonging to the child</u> transformed into a robot.

    b) The <u>flame of the candle</u> flickered and died out.

    c) <u>The voice of my cousin</u> is very strong.

2. Draw a word web for two of these list words: **lizard, noise, scary, crooked**.

Example:

whisper   singing voice

VOICE

children sleeping   yelling loudly

3. Complete the list word on each book page.

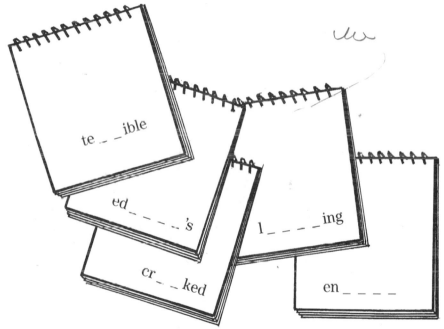

te _ _ _ ible

ed _ _ _ _ _ 's

l _ _ _ _ _ ing

cr _ _ _ ked

en _ _ _ _

4. Solve the following riddles with pairs of rhyming words. One word in each pair is a list word.

    a) Has plenty of strength _ _ _ _ _   _ _ _ _ _ _

    b) The best singer has a _ _ _ _ _ _   _ _ _ _ _

    c) Extremely frightening _ _ _ _   _ _ _ _ _

5. The most important ingredient of a scary story is a spooky setting. You have to make your reader afraid, even before anything has happened.

    a) Choose one of the settings below, or your own setting.

    b) Describe it in a very spooky way.

an old abandoned house   a dungeon   a lonesome castle

Challenges with Words

1. The prefix **super-** means 'above' or 'over'. The Super Word **superstition** literally means a 'belief standing above or over common sense'.

    Make a list of the superstitions you know. Divide your list into two columns:

Good Luck Superstitions	Bad Luck Superstitions
a four leaf clover	walking under a ladder

2. Match these other 'super-' words below with the correct meaning.

    a) superb   above the speed of sound

    b) supervise   above what is needed

    c) supersonic   above all others; highest in rank

    d) surplus   above ordinary quality; excellent

    e) supreme   in charge of others

**eerie
superstition
hero's
horrible
anxious**

3. Both plural and possessive nouns have an **s** at the end. Choose either the plural or possessive form of the word in brackets that fits the sentence.

    a) The (winds, wind's) icy breath blew through the old house.

    b) The (detectives, detective's) notes were scattered around the desk.

    c) For many (days, day's) no one had seen the creature.

    e) A strange chest had been discovered in the (castles, castle's) damp dungeon.

4. There are five synonyms for the Super Word **eerie** hidden below. How quickly can you see them in spite of the extra letters? Choose one letter from each pair of letters to find your word. For example, **weird** can be found like this: b o i s d
                                                 w e n r t

    a) u e r a s e
        t n e o c y

    b) h a r u n g m
        s t l a c l e

    c) m h n f i l p
        g a o s t u y

    d) f e u r f p l
        p i a b v u s

    e) t o r d e s y u n g
        n e l r i f c i t h

5. Brainstorm with a partner to think of some synonyms for the Super Words **anxious** and **horrible**. A thesaurus will be helpful. Write a story using as many of these synonyms as you can. Compare your story with the one your partner wrote. Now trade with another pair of classmates. You may be surprised how many different plots are created with a similar list of words.

6. New technology has its unexplained mysteries too. People talk about the bugs in their machines that cause weird things to happen.

    Write the new words that fit each clue.

    a) When everything stops and nothing can move we call it a _____ .

    b) A computer program that causes problems to occur in a computer system is called a _____ _____ .

    c) When the cursor on your computer screen stops moving we say it _____ .

computer virus

gridlock

freezes

26 Plural Possessives

children**'s**   driver**s'**

vacation
months
drivers'
hunters'
stock
rides
cattle's
building
fence
ranches'
lightning
yelling
children's
through
goes
strong

Exploring the Life of the Cowhands

Although many <u>children's</u> movies, TV shows and books are made about life on the range, the real cowhand life only lasted <u>through</u> the early days of western ranching, from 1870 to 1890. Women as well as men were cowhands and some, like Calamity Jane, became famous. Roundups were held in the spring and fall after the <u>cattle's</u> long <u>months</u> on the open range. <u>Yelling</u> and waving their hats, the cowhands would get the <u>stock</u> ready for the long trip to the rail yard. The cattle <u>drivers'</u> life was no <u>vacation</u>. A cowhand worked hard for low pay, and slept in a <u>building</u> called a 'bunkhouse'. There were many dangers on the trail. A <u>lightning</u> storm or <u>hunters'</u> gunshots could start a dangerous stampede. Nobody <u>rides</u> across the vast western plains on a horse these days, and nobody <u>goes</u> on long cattle drives. These days, most <u>ranches'</u> work is done by truck and a <u>strong</u> <u>fence</u> keeps the cattle in.

Observing Patterns

1. Complete each sentence with a list word. Write the sentences.
   a) The _____ owners branded their herd.
   b) It was time for the _____ story.
   c) The _____ bright jackets let other hunters see them in the bush.
   d) The _____ cars were being prepared for the big race.

2. Write the list words that fit these shapes.

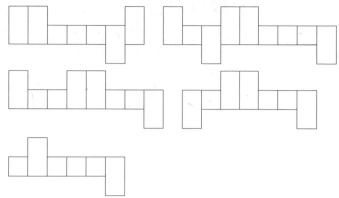

3. Write the list words that fit these clues.
   a) homophone for **stalk**
   b) surrounds a yard or field
   c) homophone for **threw**
   d) means the same as **holiday**
   e) there are twelve of them in a year
   f) rhymes with **tides**

Discovering Patterns

vacation months drivers' hunters' stock rides
cattle's building fence ranches' lightning
yelling children's through goes strong

1. Write the list words that have an apostrophe at the very end. These words are all plural. Underline the singular form of each word. How has the plural been formed in each word? What has been done to the plural form to make it mean 'belonging to'?

2. Write the two list words that end in an apostrophe and **s** (**'s**). Beside each word write the singular form. Notice that the plural is not formed by adding **s** or **es** to the base word. What has been added to the plural form to make it possessive, meaning 'belonging to'?

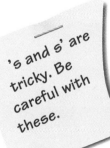

's and s' are tricky. Be careful with these.

POWERBOOSTER

- We add an apostrophe (') at the end of the plural form of most words to show possession.
- With irregular plurals, such as **children**, we add an apostrophe and **s** (**'s**) to the plural form.

123

Exploring Patterns

1. Change the words in each sentence from the singular form to the plural form.

Example: *The robin's egg lay on the ground.*
The robins' eggs lay on the ground.

a) The cat's tail swished back and forth.
b) We could hear the snake's hissing sound in the grass.
c) The look on the child's face was full of wonder.
d) The man's coat was in the closet.

2. Round up these cattle! Complete the list word on each cow.

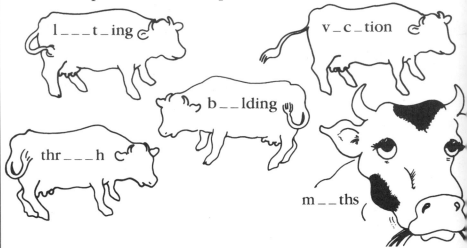

l _ _ _ t _ ing

v _ c _ tion

b _ _ lding

thr _ _ _ h

m _ _ ths

3. Complete the following sets of comparisons.
a) A vacation is like a party because _____ .
A vacation is different from a party because _____ .
b) Lightning is like a spear because _____ .
Lightning is different from a spear because _____ .
c) A building is like a box because _____ .
A building is different from a box because _____ .

4. Read this dictionary entry for the word **stock**.

stock (stok) **1** a supply or store of goods regularly kept on hand **2** cattle or other farm animals; livestock **3** shares in the ownership of a business **4** liquid in which meat or fish has been cooked, used as a base for soups and sauces.

Write the number of the definition which goes with each sentence below.
a) The rancher had purebred Hereford stock.
b) The businessperson purchased stock in that company.
c) The store has received its spring stock.
d) We used the chicken stock to make gravy.

Don't forget to proofread your ad with a partner.

SUPER WORDS

breed
dairy
herd
grazing
heifers'
domesticated

5. What's your dream holiday? Design a travel ad for a dude ranch, a wildlife safari park, marineland, or other vacation place. Choose a place where you have been or would like to go. Make it sound exciting, adventurous, and fun! Use some of these list words.

vacation   months   children's   goes

Challenges with Words

1. Match the correct Super Word to the two words which have a similar meaning. Write out the letters in the box to spell the name of a common type of milk cow.

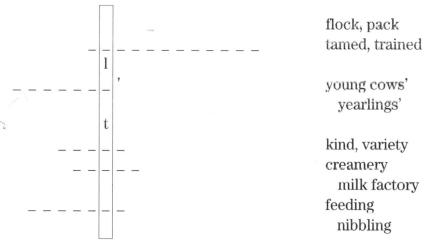

flock, pack
tamed, trained

young cows'
    yearlings'

kind, variety
creamery
    milk factory
feeding
    nibbling

2. Synonyms often show different shades of meaning. For example, the words **sip** and **slurp** both mean 'to drink', but they also tell us something about the way the drinking is done.

   a) **Grazing** is what some animals do when they eat. List five other words which describe different ways of eating.

   b) Use each of these synonyms for 'eat' in a sentence of your own.

3. Use the correct possessive word from the box in these sentences.

   a) Every day the _____ milk was collected and sent to the dairy.

   b) The sound of the _____ hooves meant that the riders had returned.

   c) All of the _____ tails were wagging furiously.

   d) The _____ foals happily trotted behind their mothers.

   e) Because of the _____ markings, they couldn't be seen.

horses'
cows'
mares'
fawns'
puppies'

4. a) Farm and ranch animals are called **domesticated** animals. Look up this Super Word in your dictionary and write down its meaning.

b) Can you list ten more domesticated animals?

WORDS IN HISTORY

> The Super Word **dairy** was once spelled **deyery**. It comes from an Icelandic word, <u>deija</u>, meaning 'a milkmaid'.

5. Dairy products come from milk. Can you guess what dairy products these are?

a) It's sometimes hard but melts in the oven.

b) When whipped, it becomes light and fluffy.

c) This dairy product tastes good on bread.

d) It's milk with all the fat removed.

e) Thick and creamy, it doesn't taste as sour as its name suggests.

6. Imagine you are staying on a ranch for the summer. Write a letter to a friend describing what it might be like. Use as many of the Super Words as you can in your letter. Don't forget to proofread.

July 16
Crazy R. Ranch

Dear Janet,
I've been at the Crazy R. Ranch for two weeks, and already I've...

27

Contractions
doesn't

doesn't
waiting
lying
photography
film
golden
spotted
haven't
slipped
they'd
stood
he'll
lay
groundhog
they're
weren't

Exploring the World of Wildlife Photography

Wildlife <u>photography</u> is a fascinating hobby that requires more than just a good camera and lots of <u>film</u>. After all, who ever heard of a moose who <u>stood</u> to pose for a picture? Wildlife photographers are used to <u>lying</u> hidden for hours, <u>waiting</u> for a bird or a <u>groundhog</u> to appear. They're careful to be still and quiet. It <u>doesn't</u> take much to alarm a wild creature, and then a <u>golden</u> opportunity has <u>slipped</u> away. Until quite recently, close-up shots of shy wild animals, such as snow leopards, <u>haven't</u> been easy to get. Now, if photographers <u>spotted</u> such a rare animal in the distance, they would switch to a telephoto lens. With this long-distance lens, <u>they'd</u> be able to get shots that <u>weren't</u> possible before. Very often, the lion that looks like <u>he'll</u> take a bite out of the camera, actually <u>lay</u> a hundred metres away when his picture was taken.

Observing Patterns

1. Write the list words that end in **-ed**. Underline the base word in each. What happens to the base word when **-ed** is added?

2. Write the six list words that fall between **debt** and **hotel** in the dictionary.

3. Write the list words that rhyme with the following words.
    stay   buying   should   dating   burnt   paid   scare

4. Which list word has two /f/ sounds but no letter **f**?

5. Write the list word that can mean either 'telling false stories' or 'resting with the body in a flat position'.

6. Write the list words that fit these shapes.

7. Write the list word that is a compound.

Discovering Patterns

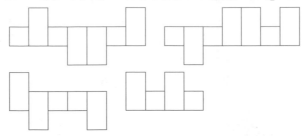

doesn't waiting lying photography film golden spotted haven't slipped they'd stood he'll lay groundhog they're weren't

1. Write the list words that are contractions. Beside each contraction, write the two words from which it is made. Think carefully about **they'd**. Notice which letter or letters have been replaced by an apostrophe.

2. Find the contractions in which the apostrophe replaces only one letter. Then make another list of the contractions in which the apostrophe replaces more than one letter.

'replaces one letter	'replaces more than one letter
she's	he'd

POWERBOOSTER

- A contraction is a shortened form of two words. One or more letters are taken out and replaced by the apostrophe ('), as in **she is—she's**.

Exploring Patterns

1. Replace each set of underlined words with a contraction.
   a) Photography is a hobby that <u>does not</u> always require expensive equipment.
   b) We <u>were not</u> planning to go to the film because we <u>have not</u> got enough money.
   c) My grandfather says <u>he will</u> pick us up after the practice.
   d) They said <u>they would</u> like to come but <u>they are</u> much too busy.

weren't

2. Good spellers are like good photographers. They often 'take pictures' of words and store them in their brains, much like photos are stored on film. These 'word pictures' of list words are incomplete. Supply the missing letters and put them back in focus!

   d _ _ sn't   w _ _ _ n't   h _ _ _ n't   _ _ ot _ gr _ _ _ y

3. The verb **lay** means 'put down; place in a certain position'. The verb **lie** means 'have one's body in a flat position along the ground or other surface'. For example, 'We **lay** the blanket on the ground so that we can **lie** on it'. In the following sentences, use the verbs **lay, laying,** or **lie, lying** correctly.
   a) The hens are _____ their eggs in the straw.
   b) We saw our friends _____ on the beach.
   c) Be sure to _____ your glasses carefully on the shelf.
   d) My cat loves to _____ on the rug by the fireplace.

129

4. You're a wildlife photographer who has just found a grizzly bear in your camp. You have two choices—to run, or take pictures. You may never get this close to a grizzly again! Choose what you would do, and explain why you made the choice you did. Compare your choice with a partner's. Did you make the same decision? Use some of these list words in your paragraph.

spotted   **he'll**   **doesn't**   **they'd**   **film**

Challenges with Words

1. Match the Super Words to the clues below.

a) When taking pictures of wildlife, you might use a _____ lens.

b) The area or location which affects living things is called its _____ .

c) _____ been gone now for nearly an hour.

d) Something which is shut in on all sides is _____ .

e) This contraction has a homophone.

f) When an image is in _____ , it's sharp and clear.

2. Here are six words and phrases that have something to do with photography. Write the opposite, or antonym, of each one.

fuzzy	dim	still life photography
distant	foreground	black and white

◢◣◢◣◢◣◢◣ WORDS IN HISTORY ◢◣◢◣

The Super Word **telephoto** was made from two Greek words: <u>tele</u>, meaning 'far off', and <u>photos</u>, meaning 'light'.

3. Can you match up these four words which begin with **tele-** to their correct meanings?

telescope   telephone   television   telemarketing

a) a system that sends and receives voices over a wire

b) selling or advertising goods or services over the telephone

c) a device that receives pictures by cable or by electronic waves through space

d) an instrument for viewing distant objects

4. Find three other **tele-** words in the dictionary and write their meanings in your notebook. What do you think the word part **tele-** means in all these words? Write a definition for **tele-** in your own words.

5. The contraction **'s** can sometimes be confusing. Here are three long forms for **'s**.

's = has   's = us   's = is

Write these sentences using the long form of **'s**.

a) Let's pack a lunch and go for a hike.

b) The hawk's gliding high above the valley.

c) The sun's been down for over an hour.

d) When it's raining, most animals find shelter.

e) Even though it's been raining, we all want to keep going.

6. a) Choose a natural environment that is familiar to you, for example, a park, a slough, the shore of a lake, or a valley.

b) If you were to make a photo album that best illustrates the environment, which photographs would you take? List six.

c) Arrange the list of your photographs in the order you think would best describe the area.

7. What's a mouse? Sometimes familiar terms are replaced by new ones and other words take on a whole new meaning. Write the words that match the definitions.

a) The term _____ _____ has replaced the term 'seeing eye dog'.

b) A list of choices in a computer program from which you can choose a topic is called a _____ .

c) A hand-held device that controls the cursor on a computer screen is called a _____ .

NEW WORDS

mouse
guide dog
menu

Suffixes
-ful -ness

thank**ful**   kind**ness**

airport
planes
wonderful
crashed
successful
minute
beautiful*
flight
happiness
fairness
thankful
radio
strangeness
faster
landed
kindness

*Beautiful is one of the 25 most frequently misspelled words.

Exploring the World of Early Flight

When we see <u>planes</u> roar in for a <u>radio</u> controlled landing at an <u>airport</u>, they seem huge and powerful. Yet the first airplane that flew was made of cloth, wires, and wood. Since it couldn't travel <u>faster</u> than a bicycle, it seems a <u>kindness</u> to even call it an airplane! Yet the 'Flyer', as this plane was called, was a <u>wonderful</u> machine. Despite the <u>strangeness</u> of its appearance, it was a <u>beautiful</u> design, and it worked. On December 17, 1903, the Flyer rose into the air, flew for less than a <u>minute</u> under its own power, and <u>landed</u> safely. Imagine the <u>happiness</u> of the inventor when Flyer was <u>successful</u> not once, but several times. In all <u>fairness</u>, the inventor had reason to be <u>thankful</u>. The wind at Kitty Hawk, where the historic flights took place, was strong and gusty. If the Flyer had <u>crashed</u>, the history of <u>flight</u> might have been quite different.

Observing Patterns

1. Unscramble the syllables in each balloon to form list words.

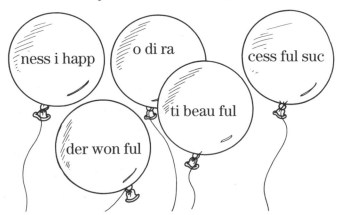

ness i happ

o di ra

cess ful suc

ti beau ful

der won ful

2. Write the list words that fit these clues.

a) three words found on the dictionary page with the guide words **every** / **found**

b) two words ending in **-ed**

c) homophone for **plains**

d) a compound word

Discovering Patterns

airport planes wonderful crashed radio successful minute beautiful flight happiness fairness thankful faster strangeness landed kindness

1. Write the list words that end in **-ful**. The suffix **-ful** makes the base word mean 'full of _____'. Therefore, a <u>careful</u> <u>person</u> is 'full of care'.

Beside each of the list words ending in **-ful**, write the base word. What happens to the base word **beauty** when **-ful** is added?

Example: thankful—thank

2. Write the list words that end in **-ness**. The suffix **-ness** makes the base word mean 'the state or quality of being _____'. Therefore, **friendliness** means 'the quality of being friendly'.

Beside each of the list words ending in **-ness**, write the base word. What happens to the base word **happy** when **-ness** is added?

Example: friendliness—friendly

POWERBOOSTER

- The suffix **-ful** means 'full of _____'. The suffix **-ness** means 'the state or quality of being _____'.
- When adding **-ful** or **-ness** to a base word ending in a consonant + **y**, change the **y** to **i**.

Exploring Patterns

1. In each pair of sentences below, the base word appears in the first one. Complete the second sentence in each pair by adding either **-ful** or **-ness** to the base word.

a) The children's eyes were full of <u>wonder</u>.
They thought the circus was _____ .
b) That was very <u>kind</u> of you.
Thank you for your _____ .
c) We enjoyed the <u>beauty</u> of the sunset.
It was a _____ sight.
d) The puppies were so <u>happy</u> to see their mother.
They showed their _____ by wagging their tails.

2. Complete the list word on each airplane.

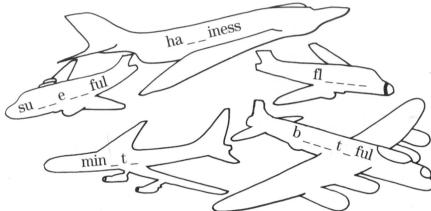

ha _ _ iness

fl _ _ _ _

su _ _ e _ _ ful

b _ _ _ _ t _ ful

min _ t _

3. Finish each set of comparisons with your own ideas.

a) An airport is like a railway station because _____ .
An airport is different from a railway station because _____ .
b) A radio is like a television because _____ .
A radio is different from a television because _____ .
c) Planes are like hot air balloons because _____ .
Planes are different from hot air balloons because _____ .

4. Use the clues to find each letter. Unscramble the letters to find a modern form of flight.

a) This letter is in **crashed** but not in **screamed**.   _
b) This letter is in **planes** but not in **plans**.   _
c) This letter is in **story** but not in **sorry**.   _
d) This letter is in **faster** but not in **fatter**.   _
e) This letter is in **minute** but not in **nighttime**.   _
f) This letter is in **tough** but not in **rough**.   _
g) This letter is in **flight** but not in **fight**.   _
Unscrambled word _ _ _ _ _ _ _

5. The invention of the airplane changed the world. Have you ever dreamed of inventing something that could change the way everyone lives, or could solve one of the world's problems? Describe an invention you'd like to see or make. Proofread your writing for spelling errors and share it with a partner. Use some of these list words in your sentences.

wonderful   successful   happiness   beautiful

Challenges with Words

1. Use the Super Words to complete the paragraph on the history of powered flight.

The year 1903 was an _____ one for aviation. It was then that the first plane was _____ and flown. It had two wings and was called a _____ . It had a _____ to help steer, and a _____ to push it forward. The first flight isn't remembered for its _____ , however, as it never reached a speed of even 20 kilometres per hour.

2. Biplanes, and planes with even more wings, were common in the early days of aviation. What would you call a plane with three wings?

3. List all the types of planes and flying craft you can think of. Check the spellings in a dictionary if you are not sure of them.

4. Add the suffixes **-ful** or **-ness** to the words in the box and complete these sentences.
  a) Be _____ to watch your step!
  b) Jet lag is a form of travel _____ .
  c) It was an exciting and _____ trip.
  d) Early jet planes were very _____ of fuel.
  e) Often an airliner's _____ is caused by poor weather and strong headwinds.

SUPER WORDS

constructed
rudder
swiftness
eventful
propeller
biplane

care
event
late
waste
weary

135

5. Both a **rudder** and a **propeller** are parts of a small aircraft. Use dictionary, an encyclopedia, or a CD-ROM on a computer, to help you match up the airplane parts to the diagram of a plane. Then write the meaning of each word you match up.

wing   fuselage   rudder   cabin
propeller   airleron   elevator   flap

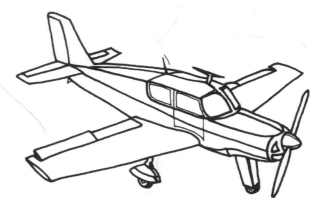

6. How many words with 3, 4, or 5 letters can you make from the Super Word **constructed**? You can rearrange the letters in any orde but do not include words with capital letters. Score one point for ea word you make and find out what type of plane you have constructe

Plane	Score
single engine plane	0 – 20
private jet	21 – 30
commercial transport plane	31 – 40
supersonic jet airliner	41 +

Why not add some of these words to your personal list?

Compound Words

backyard

someone
breakfast
probably
because*
backyard
should
training
problem
doghouse
anyone
weekend
paws
reward
tricks
calling
straight

***Because** is a frequently misspelled word.

Exploring the World of Dog Training

The dog who lives in the doghouse in your backyard needs to be trained to be a good pet. You can teach it to do tricks like fetching slippers or playing dead. More important, you should avoid having a problem pet by teaching your dog to come straight to you when you're calling it, or to keep its paws off the breakfast table. The important thing is to have someone in charge of training. If just anyone gives the dog commands, it will probably become confused and learn more slowly. In any case, training a pet takes more than a weekend. It takes a lot of time, patience, and love. A dog will learn because it wants to please you. Your praise is its reward, although sometimes a dog biscuit or two helps.

Observing Patterns

1. Write the list words that fit these shapes.

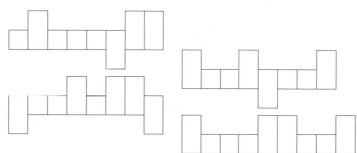

2. Write the two list words that end in **-ing**.

3. Use the base words on the doghouse to form three list words.

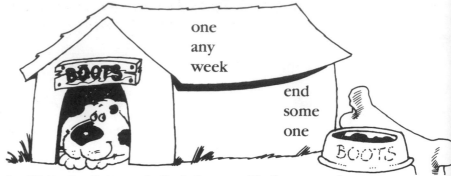

one
any
week

end
some
one

BOOTS

4. Write the list words that rhyme with these words.

sticks   would   flaws

5. Write the list words that complete these sentences.
a) Would you please help me? I have a _____ .
b) As a _____ for your good work, you can go to a movie thi[s]
evening!
c) I bought this jacket _____ it's very warm.

6. Write these words in alphabetical order.

problem
should

probably
straight

paws
someone
reward

Discovering Patterns

someone breakfast probably because backyard should training problem doghouse anyone weekend paws reward tricks calling straight

1. Write the list words that are formed by the joining of two smalle[r] words. Underline the two base words in each. We call these words **compound words**. In compound words, the two words make sense together. For example, the **weekend** is at the end of a week.

Weekend is a compound word but target is not. The two words tar and get are not related in meaning.

POWERBOOSTER

• Compound words are formed from two smaller words and have a meaning related to the smaller words.

Exploring Patterns

1. The base words below may be joined with **house** to form compound words. Complete the puzzle by selecting the correct compound word for each sentence. Look in your dictionary if you are unsure of a meaning.

hot	green	tea
boat	play	out

a) _ _ _ _ house   The children had great fun in their _____ .

b) _ _ _ house   Near the old farmhouse were some sheds and an _____ .

c) _ _ _ house   The arena was a _____ after we won the championship.

d) _ _ _ _ house   The canoes were stored in the _____ .

e) _ _ _ house   We visited a _____ when we were in Japan.

f) _ _ _ _ _ house   We can grow plants all year in a _____ .

2. Complete each comparison with a list word.

a) **Evening** is to **morning** as **dinner** is to _____ .

b) **Circle** is to **curve** as **rectangle** is to _____ .

c) **Acrobat** is to **stunts** as **magician** is to _____ .

d) **No** is to **yes** as **unlikely** is to _____ .

e) **Bad** is to **good** as **punishment** is to _____ .

3. Combine the picture clues to make compound words.

a) + = _____

b) + = _____

c) + = _____

d) + = _____

4. The list word **breakfast** has an interesting origin. **Fast** means 'to go without eating'. Explain why the morning meal would be called **breakfast**.

Can you think of compound words that begin with 'house'?

139

5. "I want a dog!" Most kids have said this to their parents at one time or another. Imagine the conversation this girl is having with he dad. What arguments will each of them use to convince the other? Work with a partner to write a short dialogue between the girl and her father. Use some of these list words.

> **should   because   probably   breakfast   someone**

You may want to use words from your personal word list in your dialogue.

Challenges with Words

1. Choose the Super Word that best fits the crazy clues below. Be careful! Some of these are tricky.

- **a)** A pet doc.
- **b)** Ken'll do.
- **c)** "In the first place," she said.
- **d)** 100% natural ingredients used in this dough.
- **e)** Its dim colour chases after you.
- **f)** "Say aah," a doctor might say.

2. A compound word like **purebred** is made of up two real words, **pure** and **bred** (the past tense of **breed**). Make as many compound words as you can with these words. For example, **cross** and **roads** make **crossroads**.

> cross   town   over   hand

3. The **greyhound** is a type of dog well known for its speed and ability to hunt. Many other dog breeds are also noted for special abilities. Use your dictionary to find out what these breeds are famous for: collie, Saint Bernard, bloodhound, Newfoundland dog, Doberman pinscher.

> **Kennel** comes from the Latin word <u>canile</u>, 'a house for dogs', which came from the Latin word <u>canis</u>, meaning 'dog'.

4. a) Do you know these other animal houses? Unscramble the animal house names in the box and match them to the animals listed below.

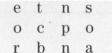

e	t	n	s	**a)**	a house for farm animals
o	c	p	o	**b)**	a home for wolves
r	b	n	a	**c)**	a house for young birds
n	d	e		**d)**	a chicken's house

b) Choose three animals and write a sentence or two explaining what kind of home they live in.

5. a) Here are four words about dogs. Write a synonym for each one.

yapping   shaggy   faithful   domesticated

b) Write four 'dog' words of your own. Challenge a partner to find a synonym for each one.

6. Imagine you are a reporter at a dog show. Write a newspaper article describing the show. Try to use as many Super Words as you can in your article. You might begin like this.

> ### LOCAL DOG CLUB RUNS OFF WITH CUP
> The Kempville Kennel Club has once again run off with most of the ribbons at this year's local dog show. The 'best in show' championship cup went to Midget, a sleek greyhound owned by...

7. The words that are combined to make the new words help make the meaning clear. **Camcorder** sounds like camera and recorder. **User-friendly** clearly means easy to use and **monorail** is a railway car that runs on one track. Mono means 'one'. Unscramble the new words in the sentences below.

a) My aunt's computer is very **srue-rlyfidne**.
b) We rode the **airlnomo** at the zoo.
c) We took our **dermacroc** with us on our vacation to make a video of our trip.

camcorder
user-friendly
monorail

STUDY STEPS

LOOK
SAY
COVER
WRITE
CHECK

Here is a list of words that may have been hard for you in Units 25–29. You and your teacher may add other words to the list.

enough	through	happiness	straight
laughing	photography	minute	they're
building	beautiful	probably	because
lightning	successful	should	months

1. Use the Study Steps for each word. Your teacher will dictate the words.

2. Complete each sentence with words from the Study List. Write the sentences in your notebook.

a) A ☐☐☐☐☐ later a bolt of ☐☐☐☐☐☐☐☐ hit the barn.

b) To be ☐☐☐☐☐☐☐☐☐☐ in the hobby of ☐☐☐☐☐☐☐☐☐☐☐ you will need ☐☐☐☐☐ of practice.

c) The ☐☐☐☐☐☐☐☐ of the children could be seen ☐☐☐☐☐☐ their ☐☐☐☐☐☐☐ smiles and ☐☐☐☐☐☐ voices.

d) You ☐☐☐☐☐ go home too ☐☐☐☐☐☐ there isn't ☐☐☐☐☐ time to play before dinner.

142

3. Unscramble the syllables to make words from the Study List.

cess ful suc   a prob bly   ness pi hap

tog phy pho ra   ti beau ful

4. Write the two-syllable words from the Study List. Put an accent (´) over the syllable that is stressed.

5. Use the possessive form to complete each of the following statements. The first one has been done for you.

    a) The bicycle belonging to the girl is the <u>girl's bicycle</u> .
        The bicycles belonging to the girls are the _____ .
    b) The coat belonging to the man is the _____ .
        The coats belonging to the men are the _____ .
    c) The toy belonging to the child is the _____ .
        The toys belonging to the children are the _____ .

6. Add the suffix **-ful** or **-ness** to the words on each square.

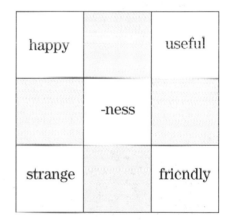

beauty		force		happy		useful
	-ful				-ness	
use		plenty		strange		friendly

7. Substitute a contraction for the underlined phrase in each sentence.

    a) The dog <u>does not</u> want to obey its owner.
    b) Are you sure you <u>have not</u> forgotten something?
    c) We <u>were not</u> successful in finding the snake's hiding place.
    d) <u>They are</u> very thankful for their wonderful friends.

Don't forget to make your own review list of difficult words.

Dictionary Skills

1. Inflected Forms: Many words that end with **-er**, **-est**, **-ed**, **-ing** will not appear as entry words in a dictionary. Instead these words will be found at the end of the entry. For example, the spelling of **occurred** will be found at the end of the entry for **occur**. It is necessary to look up the base word in such cases.

Write the entry words you would look up in order to find the following inflected forms.

laughing   happiest   slipped   scarier

2. Add the suggested ending to each base word. Check your spelling by finding the inflected form in the dictionary.

easy + est	carry + ed
happen + ing	slim + er

3. Etymology: Some dictionary entries contain information about the etymology of the word. Etymology refers to where the word comes from and the changes it has gone through in its history. The names of many animals have interesting etymologies. For example, **hippopotamus** comes from two Greek words—<u>hippo</u> meaning 'horse', and <u>potamus</u> meaning 'river'.

Find information about the etymology of these words.

porcupine   poodle   tadpole

Exploring the World of Urban Animals

<u>Animal Report Sheet</u>

NAME: <u>Raccoon</u>

SCIENTIFIC NAME: <u>Procyon lotor</u>

HABITAT: <u>Any wooded area in a city, town, or country</u>
<u>location.</u>

DESCRIPTION: <u>The raccoon has dark bands across</u>
<u>its eyes...</u>

1. Brainstorm with a partner to list wild animals that live in your region. Remember, many small wild animals live in cities and towns near people.

2. Choose one urban animal and list all of its characteristics. For example: habitat, colour, size, diet, etc. Use this list to help you write a brief report describing your animal. Use the Report Sheet at the top of the page as your model.

3. Make a list of sources you could use to find information for your report. For example: encyclopedias, magazines, newspapers, television programs, or CD-ROMs. Use some of these sources to help you write your report.

Have	
Singular	Plural
I have	We have
You have	You have
He has	They have
She has	
It has	

1. Writing with the Helping Verb Have: Some verbs are helping verbs. For example, **be**, **do**, and **have** help express the meaning of the verb more clearly.

Example: I **am** *helping you with your homework.*
           *He **did** see a bear at the camp.*
           *We **have** been to Vancouver.*

Have or **has** can be used with another verb to write about an action

- that has just happened.   I <u>have</u> just spilled my milk!

- that happened in the past and continues to happen.   He <u>has</u> lived in Halifax for six years.

Use **have** or **has** to complete the sentences.

   a) I (have, has) just remembered that man's name. It's Alex.
   b) She (have, has) lived on our street for a year.
   c) We (have, has) never seen her without her dog, Toby.
   d) It (have, has) already broken three leashes!
   e) Look! They (have, has) just bought another one.

2. Contractions can be formed with pronouns plus the word **have**. Write the contractions with **have** that fit the boxes below. The first one has been done for you.

I have | I | ' | v | e | We have   [ ][ ]'[ ]

You have [ ][ ][ ][ ]'[ ][ ]   He has   [ ][ ]'[ ]

She has   [ ][ ][ ]'[ ]   It has   [ ][ ]'[ ]

They have [ ][ ][ ][ ]'[ ]

3. Using Quotation Marks: When we write dialogue we put quotation marks (" ") around the words people say. Commas, periods, question marks, and exclamation marks, are placed **inside** the quotation marks. For example:

"Help," shouted Tiko.
"Can you throw me a rope?" he begged.
"Quick!" he shouted, "I'm sinking."

Add quotation marks to the following speeches. Remember, put the marks around just the words that are said.

a) Go home, said Toni.
b) I don't want to, his little brother cried.
c) Why not? asked Toni.
d) Because I don't want to miss all the fun! he exclaimed.

Proofing Power

Read the following paragraph with a proofreader's eye. Rewrite the sentences that need quotation marks and correct the misspelled words.

To my Aut Donna happyness is a new book on photografy. She probaly has enuf magazines and books filled with photgraphs to last her for months.

Why do'nt you throw some out"? I ask her.

Because I use them for research, Aunt Donna always answers.

She is a very successful photographer and her best pictures hang on her studio wall. You shood see them all—luaghing children, a bilding struck by lightening, beautiful sunsets. I always think their going to come to life any minite.

prehistoric

disappear

enormous

mammals

natural

middle

age

their*

there*

where*

longer

reached

fights

eaters

brain

turtle

*****Their**, **there**, and **where** are frequently misspelled words.

Exploring the World of Dinosaurs

What happened to the dinosaurs? Why did these <u>enormous</u> beasts <u>disappear</u> 65 million years ago? <u>Where</u> did they go? This is one of the great <u>prehistoric</u> mysteries of the <u>natural</u> world. Recently, scientists found a dinosaur skeleton in the <u>middle</u> of the Gobi desert, roosting on a nest of eggs. This proves some dinosaurs were warm-blooded — not cold-blooded reptiles like the <u>turtle</u> or crocodile which also lived in their time. We sometimes think of a dinosaur as a creature who <u>fights</u> and eats its victims, but many dinosaurs were <u>eaters</u> of plants. <u>There</u> are still many puzzles about the <u>age</u> of dinosaurs. One theory is that a comet or asteroid crashed into Earth, throwing up great clouds of dust. No sunlight <u>reached</u> Earth for many months, and the huge dinosaurs could no <u>longer</u> find food. The smaller, fur-covered <u>mammals</u> with a larger <u>brain</u>, were able to survive the cold and hunger.

Observing Patterns

1. Write the two list words that are homophones for one another.

2. Write the five two-syllable list words. Put an accent (´) over the stressed syllable in each word.

3. Write the list word that means 'living before recorded history'.

4. Write the list words that rhyme with the following.
    train   lights   rage   preached   there

5. Unscramble the syllables and write the list words.
    mous nor e   ap dis pear   u nat ral

6. Write the words that fit these shapes.

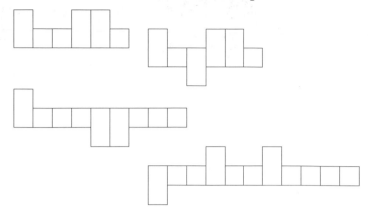

7. Write the three list words that have double consonants.

Discovering Patterns

prehistoric disappear enormous mammals natural middle age their there where longer reached fights eaters brain turtle

1. In Unit 17 we studied the schwa sound /ə/. This is the vowel sound in unstressed syllables such as in **accident** /ak´sə dənt/, **about** /ə boút/, **bottom** /bót əm/. Say the list words and look carefully at those that have the schwa sound.

2. The sound /əl/ is often found at the end of words, and can be spelled a number of ways, as **handle**, **animal**, **pencil**, and **angel**. Write the list words that end in the sound /əl/ in two columns.

/əl/ spelled **le** as in **handle**	/əl/ spelled **al** as in **animal**

POWERBOOSTER

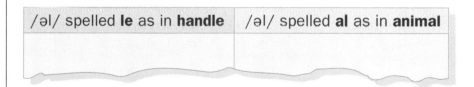

- The sound /əl/ may be spelled in a number of ways including **le** as in **handle**, and **al** as in **animal**.

Exploring Patterns

1. The list words have been written on each fossil bone using pronunciation symbols. Write each word, paying special attention to the letters which spell the schwa sound /ə/.

2. The homophones **their**, **there**, and **they're** each have a separate meaning. Use the homophone **their** when you are saying that something belongs to some people.

Example: *They brought **their** skates.*

The word **there** can be remembered because it looks like **where** and it often answers the question 'in what place?'.

Example: ***Where** are the marshmallows? They are over **there**.*

If you can trade the words **they are** in a sentence with the contractio **they're**, then the correct homophone is **they're**.

Example: ***They are** coming tonight. **They're** coming tonight.*

Complete these sentences with the correct homophone **there, th** or **they're**, and write the sentences.
a) My parents say _____ picking us up at seven o'clock.
b) All the racers brought _____ ski equipment with them.
c) Put the bananas over _____ .

3. Shrink these words so that only the base words remain.
disappear   prehistoric   eaters

4. The words in the box are all related in meaning. Choose the correct word and then write each sentence.
a) It is _____ for ducks to swim.
b) The _____ collected seven types of ferns for the study.
c) You should try to speak _____ when making a presentatior
d) We can learn valuable lessons by studying what happens in
_____ .

nature
natural
naturally
naturalist

148

5. You're digging in your garden. You throw aside rocks and wood, and suddenly you're holding a very large piece of bone. It looks like the backbone of something larger than an elephant—and elephants don't live in Canada! Write a letter to a museum telling them what you've found. Use some of the list words in your letter. You might start like this:

Dear Sir or Madam,

While digging in my backyard I found something interesting—an _____ bone. It is _____ long and weighs _____ . There are _____ and _____ on it. It looks _____ . I would like some advice about...

Challenges with Words

1. Use each Super Word correctly in the paragraph below.

Dinosaur _____ have been discovered in many areas of western Canada. These creatures, which have been _____ for millions of years, were actually _____ animals and the prairies were once covered in giant ferns and other jungle plants. From tiny shell-like beings to the _____ bones of dinosaurs, their remains have been carefully _____ from the ground and preserved in _____ .

2. The schwa sound /ə/ can be made by any vowel letter.
   a) Look up each Super Word in your dictionary and write its phonetic spelling.
   b) Underline the words that have the schwa sound.
   c) Write two more words which have the schwa sound for the letters **e** and **o**.

SUPER WORDS

extinct
tropical
museums
fossils
removed
gigantic

Ex- means 'out of' or 'former'. Re- means 'again'.

3. Both **ex-** and **re-** are prefixes. Sometimes two different prefixes can be used with the same base word. Add the prefixes **ex-** and **re-** to the five words below. Use the words you have made to complete these sentences.

port   press   cite   claim   pose

a) I like to _____ my feelings by writing poetry.

b) The teacher asked me to _____ the poem I had learned.

c) Do you have anything new to _____ ?

d) I'm going to the office to _____ the money I lost.

e) Make sure you _____ the plants to lots of light.

4. **Tropical** describes a region that is hot and wet near Earth's equator. How many other kinds of regions do you know? Match the regions in the box to their meanings.

forest
arctic
prairie
alpine
desert
coastal

a) a mountainous region

b) the region around the ocean's shore

c) a region with very little water and few plants and animals

d) the region at or near the North Pole

e) a flat or rolling land region with grass but few trees

f) a region covered with trees

WORDS IN HISTORY

The Super Word **gigantic** means 'more than simply big'. It comes from the Latin word <u>gigas</u>, the name of the land of giants in Roman legends.

5. **a)** Think of something **gigantic** and list ten words which descri

b) Using the words you have chosen, write a paragraph about y 'gigantic' topic.

6. These new words are created by combining two ideas into one compound word. Choose the correct new word to complete each sentence.

a) We slid down the _____ _____ .

b) The _____ _____ sped across the calm lake.

c) The water from the _____ _____ splashed on to the de

NEW WORDS

jet ski
wave pool
water slide

150

32

Capital Letters

Thursday

calendar
countries
again*
Wednesday
heads
means
January
Monday
July
older
August
since
November
Thursday
taken
June

*Again is one of the 25 most frequently misspelled words.

Exploring the History of Words

Some of the names on our <u>calendar</u> have curious histories coming from different <u>countries</u>. Did you know, for example, that <u>January</u> was named after Janus, a Roman god with two <u>heads</u>? His two faces looked in opposite directions. Juno, Roman goddess of marriage, gave her name to <u>June</u>. <u>July</u> and <u>August</u> were named after two Roman emperors, Julius and Augustus. <u>Since</u> <u>November</u> was the ninth month in early Roman times, its name was <u>taken</u> from the Latin word *novem*, which <u>means</u> 'nine'. Our month names are <u>older</u> than our names for the days of the week. In ancient times, each of the seven days was dedicated to a god or goddess. For example, <u>Monday</u> was the day named for the goddess of the moon; <u>Wednesday</u> for Woden, chief of the Norse gods; and <u>Thursday</u> for Thor, Norse god of Thunder.

Observing Patterns

1. Write the list words that fit these clues.
   a) end in **-day**
   b) opposite of **tails**, **younger**, **given**
   c) rhyme with **rinse**, **jeans**, **soon**
   d) are plurals

2. Find the list words that are the names for months, then write them in the order in which they appear on a calendar.

3. Unscramble the syllables to find these list words.

vem ber No   dar cal en   ar Jan y u

4. Write these words and place an accent (´) over the syllable that is stressed.

August   **July**   **again**   **countries**

5. Write the list words that fit these shapes.

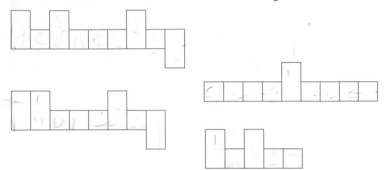

6. Write the list word with four syllables.

Discovering Patterns

calendar countries again Wednesday heads means January Monday July older June August since November Thursday taken

1. Look at the words and notice which ones have capital letters. Divide the list words that begin with capital letters into the following categories.

Days of the Week	Months of the Year

152

Exploring Patterns

1. The days of the week that are not on your list also have interesting histories. Use a dictionary to help you complete the chart for **Tuesday**, **Friday**, and **Saturday**. An example has been done for you.

Day	Comes from this language	Meaning in the old language	Named after
Sunday Tuesday Friday Saturday	Old English	day of the sun	the sun

2. Find the list words that complete the blanks, then write the completed paragraph.

Every Jan _ _ _ y first s _ _ _ _ I can remember, I have t _ _ _ _ a cal _ nd _ r for the new year and I have circled the birthdays of all my family and friends. My mom's birthday is A _ g _ _ _ third, which is on a W _ _ _ _ _ day this year. She says she doesn't like her birthday because it m _ _ _ she's another year _ _ _ er!

3. Design a word pole that tells about the word **Monday**. You may describe how that day makes you feel, or what you usually do. *Example:*

```
        M
  S O C C E R
        N
        D
        A
        Y
```

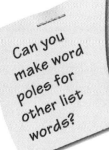
Can you make word poles for other list words?

4. Complete these comparisons, then write the list words that fit the blanks.

a) **Sunday** is to **Monday** as **Tuesday** is to _____ .

b) **August** is to **September** as _____ is to **February**.

c) **Mayors** are to **cities** as **prime ministers** are to _____ .

d) **Maybe** is to **perhaps** as **once more** is to _____ .

5. Do you think the Romans who named the months imagined their names lasting this long? Suppose you have just been named Commissioner of Months. You have to dream up new names that will last until the year 4000. You could use—

- Names of food: <u>June</u> becomes <u>Strawberry</u>, or
- Names of sports: <u>September</u> becomes <u>Footballer</u>, or
- Any other category of words you like—animals, birds, flowers.

Just remember, you have to keep everyone happy!

Challenges with Words

1. Use the Super Words to complete the paragraph on the origins of our modern calendar.

Our calendar dates back to the ones used by the ancient _____ rulers. Originally it had ten months and was sixty days short of a _____ year. Two extra months, January and _____ , were soon added. However, the calendar was still not very accurate. After several hundred years, the autumn _____ (normally on September 22) happened in July, and the winter _____ (normally on December 21) came in _____ .

WORDS IN HISTORY

The month of **February** was named after <u>Februa</u>, a Roman festival of purification or cleansing which took place in that month.

2. What important event takes place every four years in **February**? Write a sentence explaining why you think this event is important for our calendar.

Use your personal list as a source of interesting names for months.

SUPER WORDS

February
solar
September
Roman
solstice
equinox

154

My cubiculum

3. Many other English words have come from Latin, the language of the ancient Romans. For example, the Latin word <u>hortus</u> meant 'a small garden'. Our English word **horticulture** means 'the science of growing plants'.

a) Match up these other Latin words to the English words they are related to:

Latin	English
domus	culinary
aqua	aquarium
culina	cubicle
tabula	domestic
cubiculum	table

b) Now see if you can match the original Roman meanings to the Latin words above.

a kitchen _____

a house _____

a small bedroom _____

an office area _____

a channel for transporting water _____

━ ▰ ━ ▰ ━ ▰ ━◢WORDS IN HISTORY▰━ ▰ ━ ▰ ━

The word **equinox** comes from two Latin words <u>aequus</u>, meaning 'equal', and <u>nox</u>, meaning 'night'. At the equinoxes (March 21 and September 22), all places on Earth have days and nights of exactly twelve hours each.

4. The **solstices** and **equinoxes** are special times of the year. In most cultures, many holidays and festivals occur on or around these dates. In Roman times, the religious festival of **Saturnalia** was celebrated from December 17 to 23, during the time of the winter **solstice**.

a) What special holidays can you think of which take place around the **solstices** or **equinoxes**? Write down one or two events for each time of year.

b) Choose one of these special festivals and write a paragraph describing what this holiday is like.

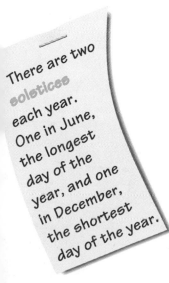

There are two solstices each year. One in June, the longest day of the year, and one in December, the shortest day of the year.

33

Related Words
sign — signal

pyramid
decide
signal
business
rectangle
sign
decision
southern
busy
south
young
bank
blocks
youth
thieves
layer

Exploring the Pyramids

The pyramids of Egypt were built as tombs for the Pharaohs, or kings of ancient Egypt. The <u>young</u> Pharaoh would <u>decide</u> where he wanted his <u>pyramid</u> to stand. He made the <u>decision</u> in his <u>youth</u> because the <u>business</u> of building a pyramid was a lifetime task. Egyptian farmers built the huge tombs on the west <u>bank</u> of the Nile River when they weren't <u>busy</u> in the fields. All of the great pyramids are near Cairo. There are none in <u>southern</u> Egypt, but <u>south</u> of Cairo, at Luxor, are the fabulous underground tombs of the Valley of the Kings. The largest pyramid is made of more than two million huge stone <u>blocks</u>. <u>Layer</u> upon layer of them rise from a base shaped like a <u>rectangle</u> to a point 137 metres high. The Pharaoh's death was the <u>signal</u> to fill the pyramid with everything he would need in his afterlife. Unfortunately, <u>thieves</u> have broken into all the pyramids, leaving no <u>sign</u> of the treasures that once lay within.

Observing Patterns

1. Write the six list words that have two syllables. Place an accent (´) over the syllable that is stressed.

2. Write the list word that is the plural of **thief**.

3. Write the list words that match these pictures.

a)   b)   c)

d)   e)   f)

4. Write the list words that rhyme with the following.

mouth   tooth   dizzy   vision   hung

5. Many words in English like **bank** are homographs. Read the three meanings of **bank** below. Write **bank¹**, **bank²**, or **bank³** for each sentence that follows.

bank¹   a long pile or heap; the ground bordering a river.

bank²   a place for keeping money.

bank³   a row or close arrangement of things.

a) There was a **bank** of snow as high as the fence.
b) A **bank** of switches controlled the lights.
c) Our **bank** has a special youth savings account.
d) The **bank** of the river was slippery and steep.

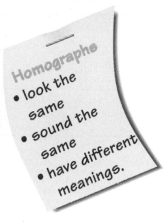

Homographs
• look the same
• sound the same
• have different meanings.

Discovering Patterns

pyramid decide signal business sign
rectangle decision southern busy south
young bank blocks youth thieves layer

1. Write the five pairs of words that are related in meaning and spelling. In each pair, underline the word that is the base word. The other word is called a **derived** word, since it is made from, or derived from, the base word.

2. Say each base word aloud and then the related word. Notice changes in pronunciation between the base word and the derived form.

In English, when two words are related in meaning, they are usually related in spelling. This important fact will help you to spell many difficult words. For example, knowing how to spell **signal** will help you to remember the silent **g** in **sign**. Even though **south** and **southern** are pronounced differently, the first vowel is spelled **ou** in both words.

POWERBOOSTER

• Words which are related in meaning are usually related in spelling. For example, **believe, belief; add, addition**.

Exploring Patterns

1. Complete each sentence below using either the base word or the derived form to fill in the blanks.

a) Always _____ to turn a corner. (sign, signal)

b) I am extremely _____ helping with our family's _____. (busy, business)

c) Many Canadians travel to _____ climates in the winter. (south, southern)

d) I know it is hard to _____ but you must make a _____ soon. (decide, decision)

2. There are many phrases in English which use the word **sign**. Imagine you have a new classmate who has just arrived in Canada and is trying to learn our language. Complete the sentences below with **sign** to help your new friend. Use a dictionary if you need help.

sign off   **sign up**   **sign in**   **sign out**

a) You _____ _____ for an activity such as soccer.

b) You _____ _____ when you arrive at work.

c) You _____ _____ when you are a radio announcer and have finished for the day.

d) You _____ _____ when you leave the building.

3. Write each of these list words so that they tell about the meaning of the word.

pyramid   **blocks**   **rectangle**

Example:

circle circle circle circle circle circle circle circle

4. Find the missing letters and write the list words on the clay tablets.

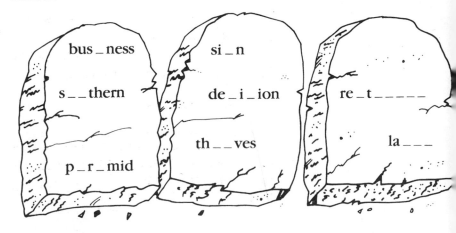

bus _ ness

s _ _ thern

p _ r _ mid

si _ n

de _ i _ ion

th _ _ ves

re _ t _ _ _ _ _

la _ _ _

5. It's cool and dark inside the great pyramid of King Khufu of Egypt. You're headed for the King's Chamber, a secret burial room. The air smells stale and musty. All at once you hear a sound! You know the tomb is empty, but still, you strain through the darkness to see...

Write a few sentences describing what you think you might see inside the Great Pyramid. Use some of these list words and some imaginative words of your own.

thieves   **pyramid**   **sign**   **young**   **decision**

Challenges with Words

1. Choose the Super Word from the word pairs that correctly fits the sentence.

a) Egyptian Pharaohs were mummified in order to (preserve, preservation) their bodies.

b) The mummies which have been discovered are in an excellent state of (preserve, preservation).

c) The (govern, government) of ancient Egypt was ruled by the Pharoah.

d) Hatshepsut, a female Egyptian ruler, was able to (govern, government) along with her son, Thutmose III, for twenty years.

e) It was a difficult (site, situation) to be suddenly faced with.

f) Giza is the (site, situation) of ten great pyramids of Egypt.

preserve
preservation
govern
government
site
situation

◀ **WORDS IN HISTORY** ▶

The Super Word **preserve** comes from the Latin words <u>pre-</u> meaning 'before', and <u>servare</u> 'to keep'. **Preserve** means 'to keep from harm'.

159

2. **Pre-** is a common prefix in English, and it still means 'before'. See if you know these **pre-** words. Match the words in the box to **pre-** in the sentences below.

school
paid
view
cautions
fabricated

a) The goods were sent <u>pre_____</u> by parcel post.

b) They bought a <u>pre_____</u> cabin and built it in a day.

c) The builders of the pyramids took many <u>pre_____</u> against thieves.

d) They needed to <u>pre_____</u> the plans before construction began.

e) <u>Pre_____</u> children can attend day-care centres.

3. A pyramid has four triangular sides. Solve each side of the pyramid puzzle by using the numbered clues. All the words in the puzzle can be made from the letters of the Super Word **situation**.

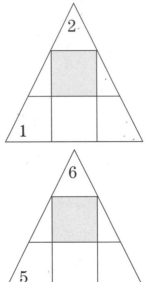
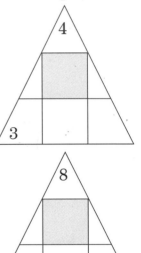

Across	Down	Up
1. short for King Tutankhamen	**2.** a negative word	**1.** You get this from #5 up.
3. a male child	**4.** a silver-white metal	**3.** You do this on a chair.
5. the past of #3 up	**6.** an almond one	**5.** sounds like #3 across
7. opposite of in	**8.** a little child	**7.** a grain

4. Many new words are needed to avoid bias. For example, **server** has replaced **waitress** or **waiter**.

Write the new word that replaces:

a) businessman

b) bag ladies

c) chairman

160

34 -ought Words

brought

apartment
brought
program
basement
specially
writing
video
until
keyboard
movement
started
entertainment
bought
battles
fought
thought

Exploring the Microcomputer

Did you know that the computer has shrunk from a unit the size of an apartment to the size of a shoe box in less than thirty years! Who would have thought it was possible? It wasn't until the invention of the transistor, and later the microchip, that the means existed of making computers smaller. By the early 1970s, basement inventors could buy these chips in an electronic supply store. They brought together inexpensive electronic parts and started producing what we now call the microcomputer. They bought a keyboard and a video display to make their computers complete. All that was needed was the writing of a program to instruct the new computers. Now microcomputers are specially useful. They control robot machines in factories, and the movement of alien spaceships in battles fought for our entertainment in computer games.

Observing Patterns

1. Write the two list words that are the same except for one letter.

2. Unscramble the syllables to find the list words.

   ly cial spe   o vid e   part a ment

3. Complete each set with a list word.
   a) cellar   attic   den
   b) monitor   printer   disk drive
   c) listening   speaking   reading
   d) action   motion   going

161

4. Write the list words that go with these pictures.

5. Write the five list words that would be found between these words in a dictionary.

problem / usually

6. a) Which list words have three syllables?
   b) Which list word has four syllables?

Discovering Patterns

apartment brought program basement specially writing video until keyboard movement started entertainment bought battles fought thought

1. Write the list words that rhyme with **not**. These four words belong to the same family since they rhyme and have the same spelling pattern.

2. Write the list words that end in **-ment**. When added to a base word, the suffix **-ment** makes the word a noun.

Knowing the spelling and the meaning of base words and suffixes can help you with derived forms. For example, the **basement** is the **base** of a house.

You may want to add some other -ment words to your list.

POWERBOOSTER

> • The sound /ot/ is spelled **-ought** in words like **bought** and **fought**.

Exploring Patterns

1. Complete the list words displayed on the computer monitor.

```
b _ s _ ment          vid _ _          unt _ _
th _ _ _ _ t          _ _ iting        _ part _ _ _ _
m _ v _ ment          br _ _ _ _ _     k _ _ b _ _ rd
```

2. Add the suffix **-ment** to each base word on the printout to make a noun. Then use your new words to write the complete sentences.

```
°   amuse
°   enjoy
°   pay
°   punish
°   announce
°
°
```

a) The convicted thief wondered what his _____ would be.
b) The students were eager to hear the _____ about the basketball game.
c) You may make your _____ at the cashier's desk.
d) We visited a wonderful _____ park on our vacation.
e) The children got so much _____ from the magic show.

3. Use the list words ending in **-ought** in sentences. You may use more than one of the words in the same sentence.

4. Use the letters of the word **entertainment** to compute as many small words as you can. Score 2 points for every two-letter word, 3 for every three-letter word, and so on. Calculate your score to see what kind of word computer you are.

Microcomputer   = 0 – 40
Minicomputer   = 41 – 80
Electronic Brain. All systems go!   = 81 +

5. Design word webs for the list words below. You may use any word that is connected in some way with the centre word.

```
   video            writing            apartment
```

163

Have your partner proofread your program.

6. If you had your own computerized robot, what task would you like to program it to do? Maybe you'd like it to make your bed, or cut the grass. List the steps you would need to include in your program. For example:

1. open garage door

2. take out lawn mower

3. check lawn for rocks etc.

Test your program on a partner. See if you can spot any steps that were left out.

Challenges with Words

1. Use the Super Word that best fits each sentence below.

a) A computer is an _____ device that stores and retrieves information.

b) We use _____ to help operate and instruct a computer.

c) We used a computer to record the data for our science

_____ .

d) Sometimes a computer seems very _____ as it silently does its calculations.

e) Everyone watched the display on the video _____ .

f) The microcomputer is _____ thousands of pieces of information a second.

monitor ✓
software
processing ✓
experiment
electronic ✓
thoughtful ✓

WORDS IN HISTORY

Software is an invented or 'coined' word that refers to the set of instructions not built into a computer. It is made up of two words—**soft** (not hard like the electronic parts) and **ware** (anything made to be sold).

164

2. When you combine the following letters, you can spell 4 five-letter words. Add the suffix -**ment** to every word and they will fit the definitions below.

a a a d e e e g j m r s s t t t u u

a) (trick or ?) + **ment** = a way of curing a disease

b) (starts with **j**) + **ment** = a decision from a judge

c) (starts with **a**) + **ment** = pleasure or fun

d) (starts with **st**) + **ment** = an account or report

3. See if you know these other 'coined' words. Combine two words from the following list and match them to their meanings.

~~tray~~ ~~chip~~ ~~copy~~ ~~hard~~ ~~ash~~

~~up~~ ~~micro~~ photo ~~ware~~ ~~pick~~

a) A kind of printed reproduction is a _____ .

b) A small truck with an open back is a _____ .

c) A container for ashes is an _____ .

d) A tiny electronic wafer is called a _____ .

e) The mechanical or electronic parts of a computer are called its _____ .

4. Here are some more computer words. Look them up in your dictionary and write their meanings in your notebook.

program   monitor   bit   byte   RAM   floppy disk

5. **a)** Computers use special number codes when processing information. They are called **ASCII** codes. ASCII stands for **A**merican **S**tandard **C**ode for **I**nformation **I**nterchange. Use the ASCII codes below to decode this sentence about computers.

84 72 69   70 73 82 83 84   70 85 76 76 89

69 76 69 67 84 82 79 78 73 67   67 79 77 80 85 84 69 82

87 65 83   67 65 76 76 69 68   69 78 73 65 67 46

ASCII Code	46	65	66	67	68	69	70	71	72	73	74	75	76	77
Character	.	A	B	C	D	E	F	G	H	I	J	K	L	M
ASCII Code	78	79	80	81	82	83	84	85	86	87	88	89	90	
Character	N	O	P	Q	R	S	T	U	V	W	X	Y	Z	

b) Now try writing a few sentences using some of the Super Words. Put your sentences into ASCII code and see if a partner can decode them.

eniac,

STUDY
STEPS

LOOK
SAY
COVER
WRITE
CHECK

Here is a list of words that may have been hard for you in Units 31–34. You and your teacher may add other words to the list.

again	their	business	until
where	there	layer	brought
disappear	countries	excitement	middle
Wednesday	decision	thought	writing

1. Use the Study Steps for each word. Your teacher will dictate the words.

2. Complete each sentence with words from the Study List. Write the sentences in your notebook.

    a) Instead of leaving in the _____ of the movie, I waited _____ it was over.

    b) There was a lot of _____ because the children had _____ favourite toys from home.

    c) _____ did the rabbit go when the magician made it _____ ? I _____ that _____ must have been another _____ of pockets in his coat.

    d) On _____ we made the _____ to visit some _____ in Europe this summer. We enjoyed Europe last year and want to go there _____ .

    e) Lian is _____ a story about the _____ she would like to start when she is older.

3. Write the study words that fit these shapes.

4. Write the study words that have two syllables. Put an accent (´) over the syllable that is stressed.

5. Write the base word for each of these study words.

disappear   excitement   writing   countries   business

6. Complete each word on the wheel with the letters that spell the sound /əl/ as in coup**le**.

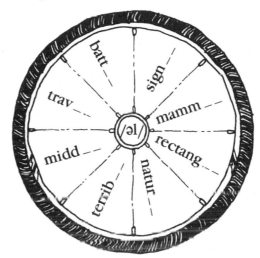

7. Explode these words by adding prefixes, suffixes, plural endings, and so on.

appear   sign   excite

Example: *natural*   *unnatural*
                    nature
            naturalist   *naturally*

8. Find the missing letters that would complete these review words. Pay special attention to the schwa /ə/ vowels in the unstressed syllables.

enorm _ _ s   dis _ pp _ _ r   f _ _ ght
cal _ nd _ r   bus _ ness   _ nt _ l
e _ _ it _ ment   Wed _ _ _ day   nat _ r _ l

Dictionary Skills

1. Idioms: Dictionary entries often include idioms or expressions. The following idioms all involve the word **head**.

Idiom	Meaning
go to one's head	make one conceited
hang one's head	be ashamed and show it
heads up	be careful, watch out
keep one' s head	stay calm

Complete each sentence with one of the expressions. You will need to adjust the words to fit the sentence.

a) They _____ in shame when they were caught cheating.

b) _____ ! The principal's coming.

c) Don't let three wins _____ .

d) It's important to _____ when the game begins.

2. a) Brainstorm idioms or expressions related to the word **heart**. Check the dictionary when you run out of ideas.

b) Use four of these expressions in sentences.

Exploring the Wilderness

1. Without electricity and running water, life would certainly be different. Make a list of all the things you might need if you were to live in a world without these modern conveniences. For example: wood stoves, fuel (wood or coal), a well or spring, hand tools, candles, etc.

2. Imagine you are living in the wilderness, far from hydro and telephone lines. Write a letter describing your life to a friend living in a modern city or town.

3. Proofread your letter. Check carefully to make sure your spelling and punctuation are correct.

Grammar Power

1. Special Verb Forms: Some verbs use a special form with the helping verb **have**.

Example: They **eat** *lunch everyday at 12 o'clock.*
             They **have** *eaten all the apples.*

Match the verbs with their special forms.

fly	written
be	gone
write	flown
go	sung
speak	been
drive	spoken
sing	driven

2. Use some of the verbs above to complete these sentences.

a) She has _____ to Japan for the summer.

b) They have _____ English all their lives.

c) We have already _____ to that movie twice!

d) My sister has just _____ her new car around the block.

e) You have _____ that song so many times my head aches.

3. Writing Paragraphs: A paragraph is a signal to the reader. It means a change in speaker, or a new thought. Indent the first line of a new paragraph to show this change.

In the following piece of writing there are no paragraphs, and it is hard to tell who is speaking. Rewrite the piece, beginning a new paragraph each time the speaker changes.

"Can you come to my house tonight?" José asked his friend, Fernando. "I don't think so," Fernando sighed. "Why not?" José wanted to know. "I have to look after my little brother." "That's too bad," José said. "I have a new video game I wanted to show you."

4. Making Comparisons: Some adjectives have special comparative and superlative forms.

Word	Comparative	Superlative
good	better	best
bad	worse	worst
far	farther	furthest
little	less	least

Use these special forms and your own ideas to state your opinions.

a) I think tomato soup is _____ food, a chicken sandwich is _____ , and pizza is the _____ .

b) I think rainy weather is _____ , a thunderstorm is _____ , and a hurricane is the _____ .

c) I have _____ interest in skiing, _____ in tennis, and the _____ in golf.

Proofing Power

Proofread the following paragraph and correct all the errors you can find.

On Wednesday, my friend Alycia and I went to her mom's office in the midle of the city. We pretended we had our own buisness and had fun riting letters to our clients in many countrys. We stayed untill lunchtime and then went to a nearby restrant. In all the excitement, I forgot to bring my wallet. I thoght I had bruoght it with me, but I must have left it at home. When the bill came, I wanted to diappeare! I made the decission right then and there that I'd never forget it agen.

Basic Word List

aboard	become	chain	discovered
accident	bees	chase	disease
addresses	before	cheap	display
adventures	beginning	children's	diver
Africa	believed	chimney	doctors
again	beneath	circle	doesn't
against	berries	classes	doghouse
age	bicycle	cliff	drank
ahead	blocks	clothing	dreaming
airport	blue	coaches	drew
Alberta	body	coal	dried
already	bones	coming	drivers'
America	bought	complete	dropped
amount	brain	continent	dumb
anyone	breakfast	continue	during
anyway	bright	copper	
apart	British	countries	earliest
apartment	brought	country	earth
appear	building	cousins	eastern
Arctic	bulldozer	court	eaters
area	bunches	crashed	editor's
argue	buried	crew	eerie
arms	business	crooked	eighteen
arrived	busy		electric
athlete		dangerous	eleven
attack	calendar	darkness	enemies
attacked	Calgary	death	energy
August	calling	decide	enormous
	camper	decision	enough
backyard	Canada	deer	entertainment
bank	captain	deposits	equipment
base	captive	describe	especially
basement	carefully	desert	everywhere
battles	carried	difficult	example
beam	carry	digging	except
bean	cattle's	directions	excited
beautiful	cells	dirt	explodes
because	certain	disappear	exploring

fail	groundhog	kilometres	medical
fairness	groups	kindness	melt
famous	growing	kinds	metal
faster	guard	knew	Mexico
father's	guide	knives	microscope
feeling		known	middle
female	hair		millions
fence	handle	landed	minute
fifth	hands	larger	missing
fights	happiness	laser	modern
film	haven't	laughing	Monday
finally	having	lay	months
finds	he'll	layer	motor
fixed	heads	least	mountain
flashlight	heat	lens	movement
flight	herself	lightning	muscle
flower	hiding	line	
follow	highway	lives	natural
forever	hockey	lizard	noise
forty	hold	loaded	north
fought	hover	locate	notice
four	huge	locked	November
frightened	hunters'	log	
front	husband	longer	objects
furniture		longest	offensive
furry	iceberg	loose	officer
future	include	luck	often
	information	lying	oil
gait	instead		older
gentle	instruments	machine	Olympics
geography	interested	main	order
glue		making	organized
goal	January	male	outdoors
goes	jewels	mammals	oxygen
golden	journey	Manitoba	
gorilla	July	mapped	painter's
grabbed	June	married	pair
greatly		matches	pants
grip	keyboard	means	passed

pause
paws
pedal
people
perhaps
photograph
photography
picture
pieces
pilot
pioneer
plains
planes
planets
player
points
pollution
possible
practice
prehistoric
probably
problem
program
promise
purring
pyramid

quarter
quickly
quiet
quietly
quit

radio
ranches'
reached
reaches

reason
receive
rectangle
reduce
remain
remarkable
remembered
replied
return
reward
rides
right
robot
rules

Saskatchewan
scary
scene
science
score
search
searches
seat
seemed
sending
serve
shoot
shore
should
sign
signal
silently
since
size
skill
skull
slipped

slowly
smoke
solid
someone
south
southern
spaceship
special
specially
speed
spike
spirals
spooky
sport
spotted
stalk
started
states
station
stayed
stepped
stock
stood
straight
strangeness
strong
style
successful
suddenly
suit
support
supreme
surface
surprise

taken
teachers

telescope
temperature
terrible
thankful
their
there
they'd
they're
thieves
though
thought
through
throw
thumb
Thursday
tiny
toward
tracked
traffic
trail
training
travel
treasures
tricks
trophy
turtle
twenty-five
twice

unattractive
understand
unexplored
unfashionable
unfinished
unidentified
unpacked
until

unusual
usually

vacation
valleys
Vancouver
video
village
voice
volleyball

waiting
warmest
watched
waves
wearing
weather
Wednesday
weekend
weren't
where
whiskers
whole
without
wonderful
worked
worst
writer's
wrote

yelling
young
youth

MINI–DICTIONARY

▼▼▼▼▼▼▼▼

a	hat, cap	**i**	it, pin	**p**	paper, cup	**z**	zero, breeze
ā	age, face	**ī**	ice, five	**r**	run, try	**zh**	measure, seizure
ä	barn, far			**s**	say, yes		
				sh	she, rush	**ə**	represents:
b	bad, rob	**j**	jam, enjoy	**t**	tell, it		a in about
ch	child, much	**k**	kind, seek	**th**	thin, both		e in taken
d	did, red	**l**	land, coal	**ŦH**	then, smooth		i in pencil
		m	me, am				o in lemon
		n	no, in				u in circus
e	let, best, care	**ng**	long, bring	**u**	cup, butter		
ē	equal, be			**u̇**	full, put		
ėr	term, learn			**ü**	rule, move		
		o	hot, rock	**yü**	use, music		
		ō	open, go				
f	fat, if	**ô**	order, door	**v**	very, save		
g	go, bag	**oi**	oil, voice	**w**	will, woman		
h	he, how	**ou**	house, out	**y**	young, yet		

A ▼▼▼

a·board [ə bôrd'] **1** on board; on, in, onto, or into a ship, train, bus, aircraft, etc.: *All the passengers went aboard.* **2** onto or into: *They went aboard the ship.* **1** *adv.,* **2** *prep.*

ac·ci·dent [ak'sə dənt] something harmful or unlucky that happens unexpectedly and apparently by chance: *He was killed in an automobile accident.* *n.*

a·cid rain [as'id rān] rain or snow contaminated by acids formed when industrial pollutants undergo chemical changes in the atmosphere.

ad·dress [ə dres'; *also* ad'res *for* 2] **1** use a title in speaking or writing to: *How do you address a mayor? The Queen is addressed as 'Your Majesty'.* **2** the place at which a person, business, etc. may be found or reached: *Send the letter to her business address.* **1** *v.,* **2** *n.*

ad·ven·ture [ad ven'chər] **1** a bold and difficult undertaking, usually exciting and somewhat dangerous: *White-water rafting is an adventure.* **2** an unusual experience: *The trip to Québec City was an adventure for us.* *n.*

a·gain [ə gen' *or* ə gān'] another time; once more: *Come again to play. Say that again.* *adv.*

a·gainst [ə genst' *or* ə gānst'] **1** in opposition to: *She spoke against the suggestion.* **2** upon: *Rain beats against the window.* **3** in preparation for: *Squirrels store up nuts against the winter.* **4** in defence from: *A fire is a protection against the cold.* *prep.*

age [āj] **1** a time of life: *the age of eighteen.* **2** a length of life: *Turtles live to a great age.* **3** a certain period in history: *the atomic age.* **4** grow old: *He is aging fast.* **1–3** *n.,* **4** *v.,* **aged, ag·ing.**

a·head [ə hed'] **1** in front; before: *She told me to walk ahead.* **2** in advance: *Rajiv was ahead of his class in reading.* *adv.*

air bag [er'bag] a large plastic bag in a vehicle that inflates in a collision to protect the driver and passengers from possible injury. *n.*

air miles [er' mīlz'] the privilege of travelling a given distance by air free of charge, earned by buying products or services from certain companies. *n.*

air·port [er'pôrt'] a place where aircraft regularly come to take on or discharge passengers or freight. *n.*

Al·ber·ta [al bėr'tə] (after Princess Louise *Alberta*, 4th daughter of Queen Victoria); province of Canada; capital is Edmonton. *n.*

al·read·y [ol red'ē] before this time; by this time; even now: *You are half an hour late.* *adv.*

A·mer·i·ca [ə mer'ə kə] North America, especially Canada and the United States. *n.*

a·mount [ə mount'] **1** quantity: *No amount of coaxing would make the dog leave its owner.* **2** add up; be equal: *The loss from the flood amounts to a million dollars. Keeping what belongs to another amounts to stealing.* 1 *n.*, 2 *v.*

an·y·one [en'ē wun'] anybody; any person: *Anyone in the school may come to the party.* *pron.*

an·y·way [en'ē wā'] in any case: *I am coming anyway, no matter what you say.* *adv.*

a·part [ə pärt'] **1** to pieces; in pieces, in separate parts: *The girl took the watch apart to see what made it tick.* **2** away from each other: *Keep the dogs apart.* **3** to one side; aside: *He stood apart from the others.* *adv.*

a·part·ment [ə pärt'mənt] a self-contained set of rooms to live in. *n.*

ap·pear [ə pēr'] seem; look: *The apple appeared to be fine on the outside, but it was rotten inside.* *v.*

arc·tic [ärk'tik *or* är'tik] **1** at or near the North Pole; of the north polar region: *the arctic fox.* **2 the Arctic, a** the north polar region. **b** the Arctic Ocean. 1 *adj.*, 2 *n.*

ar·e·a [er'ē ə] a level surface or space: *The playing area was marked off with white lines.* *n.*

ar·gue [är'gyü] **1** discuss with someone who disagrees: *He argued with his sister about who should wash the dishes.* **2** try to prove by reasoning: *Columbus argued that the world was round.* *v.*, **ar·gued, ar·gu·ing.**

arm [ärm] **1** the part of the human body attached at the shoulder. **2** something shaped or used like an arm: *the arm of a chair, an arm of the sea.* **3** provide with weapons; supply with any means of defence or attack. 1, 2 *n.*, 3 *v.*

ar·rive [ə rīv'] **1** come to a place: *We arrived in Kingston a week ago.* **2** come: *The time has arrived for you to study.* *v.*, **ar·rived, ar·riv·ing.**

ath·lete [ath'lēt] a person trained in exercises of strength, speed, and skill: *Baseball players and swimmers are athletes.* *n.*

at·tack [ə tak'] **1** use force or weapons to hurt; go against as an enemy: *The dog attacked the cat.* **2** an assault or attacking: *The attack of the enemy took the town by surprise.* 1 *v.*, 2 *n.*

at·trac·tive [ə trak'tiv] pleasing; winning attention and liking: *They have an attractive home.* *adj.*

Au·gust [og'əst] the eighth month of the year. August has 31 days. *n.*

B ▼▼▼

back·yard [bak'yärd'] a yard or garden behind a house: *She grows vegetables in her backyard.* *n.*

bank [bangk] **1** the ground bordering a river, lake, etc. **2** tilt when making a turn: *The pilot banked the airplane steeply.* 1 *n.*, 2 *v.*

base [bās] **1** a starting place; headquarters: *Our army established a base to store supplies.* **2** establish; found: *His large business was based on good service.* 1 *n.*, 2 *v.*, **based, bas·ing.**

base·ment [bās'mənt] the lowest storey of a building, partly or completely below ground. *n.*

bat·tle [bat'əl] **1** any fight or contest: *a battle of words.* **2** fight; struggle; contend: *The swimmer had to battle a strong current.* 1 *n*, 2 *v.*, **bat·tled, bat·tling.**

beam [bēm] **1** a ray or rays of light: *The beam from the flashlight showed a kneeling man.* **2** look or smile brightly: *Her face beamed with delight.* 1 *n.*, 2 *v.*

bean [bēn] **1** a smooth, somewhat flat seed used as a vegetable: *pork and beans.* **2** the long pod containing such seeds: *When young and fresh, green or yellow beans are cooked as vegetables.* *n.*
☛ *Homonyms.* **Bean** is pronounced like **been** [bēn].

beau·ti·ful [byü'tə fəl] very pleasing to see or hear; delighting the mind or senses: *a beautiful picture, beautiful music.* *adj.*

be·cause [bi kuz'] for the reason that; since: *Most children play ball because they enjoy the game.* *conj.*

be·come [bi kum'] **1** come to be; grow to be: *It is becoming colder. She became wiser as she grew older.* **2** seem proper for; suit; look well on: *That white jacket becomes you.* *v.*, **be·came, be·come, be·com·ing.**

bee [bē] a four-winged insect that lives in large groups and makes honey and wax: *Female bees can sting.* *n.*

be·fore [bi fôr'] **1** earlier than: *We always play games before the bell rings (conj.). I do my homework before supper (prep.).* **2** in front of; ahead of: *Walk before me.* **3** rather than; sooner than: *I'll give up the trip before I go with them (conj.). I'd take ice cream before candy (prep.).* 1, 2, 3, *prep.*, 1, 3 *conj.*

be·gin [bi gin'] **1** do the first part of; make a start. **2** come or bring into being: *The club began two years ago.* *v.*, **be·gan, be·gun, be·gin·ning.**

be·gin·ning [bi gin'ing] **1** a start: *to make a good beginning, from beginning to end.* **2** a first cause; a source; the origin: *One wrong decision was the beginning of all his misfortunes.* **3** just starting: *a beginning student.* 1, 2, *n.*, 3 *adj.*

be·lieve [bi lēv'] **1** think something is true or real: *We all believe that Earth is round.* **2** think; suppose: *I believe we are going to have a test.* *v.*, **be·lieved, be·liev·ing.**

be·neath [bi nēth'] **1** below; under; in a lower place: *What you drop will fall upon the spot beneath (adv.). The dog sat beneath the tree (prep.).* **2** unworthy of: *The proud boy thought washing dishes was beneath him.* 1 *adv.*, 1, 2 *prep.*

ber·ry [ber'ē] a small, juicy fruit, usually not having a stone: *Strawberries and currants are berries.* *n.*

bi·cy·cle [bi'sə kəl] **1** a vehicle having two wheels, one behind the other, that support a light metal frame on which there are handles and a seat for the rider: *You ride a bicycle by pushing two pedals with your feet.* **2** ride a bicycle. 1 *n.*, 2 *v.*, **bi·cy·cled, bi·cy·cling.**

block [blok] **1** a solid piece of wood, stone, metal, ice, etc.: *The Pyramids are made of blocks of stone.* **2** put things or be in the way of; obstruct; hinder the use of: *The car is blocking the driveway.* 1 *n.*, 2 *v.*

blue [blü] **1** the colour of the clear sky in daylight. **2** having this colour. 1 *n.*, 2 *adj.*, **blu·er, blu·est.**

bod·y [bod'ē] **1** the physical part of a living person, including skeleton, organs, muscles, nerves, skin, etc. **2** a dead person; corpse: *The body was found by the police.* *n.*, *pl.* **bod·ies.**

bone [bōn] **1** one of the pieces of the skeleton of an animal with a backbone: *a beef bone for soup* **2** take the bones out of: *We boned the fish before eating it.* 1 *n.*, 2 *v.*, **boned, bon·ing.**

bought [bot] the past tense and past participle of **buy**: *We bought apples from the farmer.* *v.*

brain [brān] **1** the mass of nerve cells enclosed in the skull or head of persons and animals: *The brain is used in feeling and thinking.* **2** kill by smashing the skull of: *The trapper brained the injured wolf with a large stone.* 1 *n.*, 2 *v.*

break·fast [brek'fəst] **1** the first meal of the day. **2** eat breakfast: *They breakfasted at 7:30 a.m.* 1 *n.*, 2 *v.*
☛ *Etymology.* **Breakfast** is a shortened form of an old phrase *to break one's fast.*

hat, āge, fär; let, ēqual, tėrm; it, īce; hot, ōpen, ôrder oil, out; cup, pùt, rüle; ə above, takən, pencəl, lemən, circəs ch, child; ng, long; sh, ship th, thin; ŦH, then; zh, measure

bright [brīt] **1** giving much light; shining: *The stars are bright, but sunshine is brighter.* **2** very light or clear: *It is a bright day.* **3** cheerful or lively: *a bright smile.* *adj.*

Brit·ish [brit'ish] **1** of or having to do with the United Kingdom or its people. **2** the **British**, *pl.* people of the United Kingdom. 1 *adj.*, 2 *n.*

brought [brot] the past tense and past participle of **bring**: *He brought his lunch yesterday. We were brought to school in a bus.* *v.*

build·ing [bil'ding] something built. Barns, houses, sheds, factories, and hotels are all buildings. *n.*

bull·doz·er [bùl'dō'zər] a powerful tractor that moves dirt, rocks, etc. by means of a wide steel blade attached to the front. *n.*

bunch [bunch] a group of things of the same kind growing, fastened, placed, or thought of together: *a bunch of grapes, a bunch of flowers.* *n.*

bur·y [ber'ē] put (a dead body) in the earth, in a tomb, or in the sea: *They buried the dead bird.* *v.*, **bur·ied, bur·y·ing.**

busi·ness [biz'nis] whatever one is busy at; work: *A carpenter's business is building with wood.* *n.*

bus·iness·per·son [biz'nəs pėr'sən] **1** a man or woman in business. **2** a man or woman who is good at business. *n.*

bus·y [biz'ē] working; active; having plenty to do: *A secretary is a busy person.* *adj.*, **bus·i·er, bus·i·est, bus·ied, bus·y·ing.**

C ▼▼▼

cal·en·dar [kal'ən dər] a chart showing the months and weeks of the year and the day of the week on which each date comes. *n.*

Cal·ga·ry [kal'gər ē] a city in southern Alberta, Canada. *n.*

call·ing [kol'ing] a profession, occupation, or trade: *The teacher took great pleasure in his calling.* *n.*

camp·er [kam'pər] a person who camps. *n.*

Can·a·da [kan′ə də] a large country occupying the northern part of North America except Alaska. *n.*

cap·tain [kap′tən] **1** a leader; chief. **2** lead or command as captain: *Barbara will captain the team.* **1** *n.*, **2** *v.*

cap·tive [kap′tiv] a person or animal taken and held by force, skill, or trickery: *The army brought back many captives.* *n.*

care·ful [ker′fəl] **1** thinking what one says; watching what one does; taking pains; watchful; cautious: *Be careful to tell the truth at all times.* **2** full of care or concern; attentive: *She was careful of the feelings of others.* *adj.*

car·ry [kar′ē *or* ker′ē] **1** take from one place or time to another: *Buses carry passengers.* **2** bear the weight of; hold up; support: *Those columns carry the roof.* *v.*, **car·ried, car·ry·ing.**

cat·tle [kat′əl] **1** cows, bulls, and steers; oxen. **2** farm animals; livestock. *pl.n.*

cell [sel] a very small unit of living matter. All animals and plants are made of cells, which are formed of a small amount of living matter, called protoplasm, surrounded by a very thin membrane. *n.*

cer·tain [sėr′tən] **1** sure: *It is not certain who will win the contest.* **2** definite but not named; some: *Certain plants will not grow in this country.* *adj.*

chain [chān] **1** a flexible, connected series of links or rings used for connecting or confining things, or for decoration: *The anchor was attached to a heavy steel chain.* **2** attach or confine using a chain. **1** *n.*, **2** *v.*

chair·per·son [cher′pėr′sən] **1** a person who presides at or is in charge of a meeting. **2** the head of a committee. *n.*

chase [chās] follow after to catch or kill; hunt: *The cat chased the mouse.* *v.*, **chased, chas·ing.**

cheap [chēp] low in price or cost; not expensive: *Fresh vegetables are cheap out in the country.* *adj.*

chil·dren [chil′drən] plural of **child**. *n.*

chim·ney [chim′nē] an upright structure used to make a draft for a fire and carry away smoke: *Pat's house has two chimneys.* *n.*, *pl.* **chim·neys.**

cir·cle [sėr′kəl] **1** a curved line of which every point is equally distant from a point called the centre. **2** a ring: *They danced in a circle.* **3** a group of people held together by the same interests: *the family circle; a circle of friends.* *n.*

class [klas] **1** a group of persons or things of the same kind. **2** put in a class; classify. **1** *n.*, **2** *v.*

cliff [klif] a steep, high face of rock or earth; precipice: *Great cliffs overhung the canyon.* *n.*

cloth·ing [klō′ŦHing] clothes. *n.*

coach [kōch] **1** a large, closed carriage with seats inside and, often, on top. Coaches carried passengers along a regular run, stopping for meals and fresh horses. **2** a person who teaches or trains athletes: *a football coach.* **3** train or teach: *He asked his mother to coach him in arithmetic.* **1, 2** *n.*, **3** *v.*

coal [kol] a black mineral formed in the earth from partly decayed vegetable matter that has been under great pressure for a long time: *Coal is mined for use as a fuel.* *n.*

come [kum] **1** move (toward whoever is speaking): *Come this way. One boy came toward me; the other boy went away.* **2** get near; arrive: *The train comes at noon.* *v.*, **came, come, com·ing.**

com·plete [kəm plēt′] **1** with all the parts; whole; entire: *a complete set of garden tools.* **2** finish: *She completed her homework early in the evening.* **1** *adj.*, **2** *v.*, **com·plet·ed, com·plet·ing.**

com·put·er vi·rus [kəm pyü′tər vī′rəs] a piece of code in a program or file that stops it from working properly and is very difficult to find and remove. It is originally put in as a form of sabotage, but is often passed from system to system by users who exchange disks, files, etc. without knowing about it.

con·ti·nent [kon′tə nənt] one of the seven great masses of land on the earth: *The continents are North America, South America, Europe, Africa, Asia, Australia, and Antarctica.* *n.*

con·tin·ue [kən tin′yü] keep up; keep on; go on; go on with: *We continued our work at the hospital.* *v.*, **con·tin·ued, con·tin·u·ing.**

cop·per [kop′ər] a reddish metal that is easily shaped into wire or sheets and resists rust: *Copper is a good conductor of electricity.* *n.*

cord·less [kôrd′lis] **1** without a cord. **2** of mechanical devices, battery-operated, as opposed to those that must be plugged into an outlet: *a cordless telephone.* *adj.*

coun·try [kun′trē] **1** land; a region: *The hill country to the north was rough and mountainous.* **2** nation; state: *the country of France.* *n.*, *pl.* **coun·tries.**

court [kôrt] a place marked off for a game: *a tennis court, a handball court.* *n.*

cous·in [kuz′ən]   the son or daughter of one's uncle or aunt: *First cousins have the same grandparents; second cousins have the same great-grandparents; and so on for third and fourth cousins. adj.*

crash [krash]   **1** fall to the earth or strike something in such a way as to be damaged or wrecked: *The airplane went out of control and crashed.* **2** such a fall or striking: *a car crash.* 1 *v.*, 2 *n.*

crew [krü]   the people who operate a ship, rowboat, aircraft, etc: *The entire crew of the destroyer was drowned. n.*

crook·ed [kruk′id]   **1** not straight; bent; curved; twisted: *a crooked stick.* **2** dishonest: a crooked business deal. *adj.*

D

dan·ger·ous [dān′jə rəs]   likely to cause harm; not safe; risky: *The road around the mountain is dangerous. adj.*

dark [därk]   **1** without light. *A night without a moon is dark.* **2** nightfall: *He couldn't stay out after dark.* 1 *adj.*, 2 *n.*

death [deth]   the act of dying; the ending of life in human beings, animals, or plants: *She faced death with courage. n.*

de·cide [di sīd′]   **1** settle: *Let us decide the question by tossing a coin.* **2** resolve; make up one's mind: *He decided to be a writer. v.*, **de·cid·ed, de·cid·ing.**

de·ci·sion [di sizh′ən]   the act of deciding; making up one's mind: *He had not yet come to a decision about which colour to use. n.*

deer [dēr]   one of the group of cud-chewing animals with long legs and small, split hooves, including the elk, caribou, moose, mule deer, reindeer, and white-tailed deer. *n., pl.* **deer.**

de·pos·it [di poz′it]   **1** put down; lay down; leave lying: *She deposited her bundles on the table.* **2** put in a place to be kept safe: *Deposit your money in the bank.* **3** a mass of some mineral in rock or in the ground: *deposits of coal.* 1, 2 *v.*, 3 *n.*

de·scribe [di skrīb′]   tell in words how a person looks, feels, or acts, or how a place, a thing, or an event looks; tell or write about. *v.*, **de·scribed, de·scrib·ing.**

des·ert[1] [dez′ərt]   a region with very little water and plant or animal life; barren, desolate land. *n.*

hat, āge, fär; let, ēqual, tėrm; it, īce; hot, ōpen, ôrder
oil, out; cup, pùt, rüle; əbove, takən, pencəl, lemən, circəs
ch, child; ng, long; sh, ship
th, thin; ᴛʜ, then; zh, measure

de·sert[2] [di zėrt′]   go away, and leave alone; abandon; forsake; run away from duty: *You are my friend and I will never desert you. v.*
☛ Homonyms. **Desert**[2] is pronounced like **dessert.**

desk·top [desk′top′]   of a computer; small enough to sit on a desk. *adj.*

dif·fi·cult [dif′ə kult′]   hard to do or understand: *Cutting down the tree was difficult. adj.*

dig [dig]   **1** use a shovel, spade, hands, claws, or snout to make a hole or to turn over ground: *Dogs bury bones and dig them up later.* **2** a thrust or poke: *The boy gave his friend a dig in the ribs.* 1 *v.*, **dug, dig·ging;** 2 *n.*

di·rec·tion [di rek′shən *or* dī rek′shən]   **1** guidance; management; control: *The school is under the direction of a good principal.* **2** an order or command. **3** any way in which one may face or point: *North, south, east, and west are directions. n.*

dirt [dėrt]   **1** mud, dust, earth, or anything like them: *Dirt soils skin, clothing, houses, or furniture.* **2** information about dishonourable or shameful behaviour: *Some people are always spreading dirt about others. n.*

dis·ap·pear [dis′ə pēr′]   pass from sight: *The little dog disappeared down the road. v.*

dis·cov·er [dis kuv′ər]   find out; see or learn of for the first time: *Gold was discovered in the Klondike in 1896. v.*

dis·ease [də zēz′]   sickness; illness: *People, animals, and plants are all liable to suffer from disease. n.*

dis·play [dis plā′]   **1** show; reveal: *He displayed his good nature by answering all our questions.* **2** showing; exhibition: *She did not like the boy's display of bad temper.* 1 *v.*, 2 *n.*

div·er [dī′vər]   a person whose occupation is to work under water. *n.*

doc·tor [dok′tər]   **1** a person having a licence to practise medicine or perform surgery: *a medical doctor.* **2** give medical treatment to: *She doctors her childen for ordinary colds.* 1 *n.*, 2 *v.*

does·n't [duz′ənt]   does not.

dog·house   [dog'hous']   a small house or shelter for a dog. *n.*

drank   [drangk]   the past tense of drink: *She drank her milk an hour ago.* *v.*

dream   [drēm]   **1** something one thinks or seems to feel, hear, or see during sleep or while engrossed in one's imagination. **2** have a dream. **3** think of something as possible; imagine: *The day seemed so bright I never dreamed there would be rain.* 1 *n.*, 2, 3 *v.*, **dreamed** or **dreamt, dream·ing.**

drew   [drü]   the past tense of **draw**: *He drew a picture of his father.* *v.*

dried   [drīd]   the past tense and past participle of **dry**: *I dried my hands. These clothes have been dried in the sun.* *v.*

drive   [drīv]   make go; cause to move: *Drive the flies away. She drove the cow out of the barn.* *v.*, **drove, driv·en, driv·ing.**

drop   [drop]   **1** a sudden fall: *a drop in prices. The temperature took a big drop last night.* **2** let fall: *He dropped the package.* 1 *n.*, 2 *v.*, **dropped, drop·ping.**

dumb   [dum]   not able to speak: *Even intelligent animals are dumb.* *adj.*

dur·ing   [dyü'ring *or* dü'ring]   at some time in; in the course of: *Come to see us sometime during the day.* *prep.*

E ▼▼▼

ear·ly   [ėr'lē]   near the beginning: *the early years* (adj.) *The heroine appears early in the book* (adv.). *adj. or adv.*

earth   [ėrth]   **1 Earth,** the planet on which we live, a great sphere that moves around the sun; the globe: *Earth is round. China is on the other side of the Earth.* **2** the ground: *The arrow fell to the earth 100 metres away.* *n.*

east·ern   [ēs'tərn]   in or toward the east: *an eastern province.* *adj.*

eat   [ēt]   chew and swallow: *Cows eat grass and grain.* *v.*, **ate, eat·en, eat·ing.**

ed·i·tor   [ed'ə tər]   a person who EDITS, especially one whose occuptation is preparing material for publication or broadcasting. *n.*

eight·een   [āt'tēn']   eight more than ten; 18. *n. or adj.*

e·lec·tric   [i lek'trik]   run or operated by electricity: *an electric train, an electric guitar, an electric light.* *adj.*

e·lev·en   [i lev'ən]   one more than ten; 11. *n. or adj.*

e·mail   [ē' māl']   ELECTRONIC MAIL messages sent from one terminal to another or others by users of a computer network system. *n.*

en·e·my   [en'ə mē]   **1** a person or group that hates and tries to harm another. **2** anything harmful: *Frost is an enemy of flowers.* *n., pl.* **en·e·mies.**

en·er·gy   [en'ər jē]   active strength or force; the will to work or act: *Those who exercise regularly have more energy.* *n., pl.* **en·er·gies.**

e·nor·mous   [i nôr'məs]   extremely large; huge: *Long ago there were enormous dinosaurs on Earth.* *adj.*

e·nough   [i nuf']   as much as is wanted or needed: *Has he had enough to eat?* *n.*

en·ter·tain·ment   [en'tər tān'mənt]   something that interests, pleases, or amuses, such as a show or circus. *n.*

e·quip·ment   [i kwip'mənt]   **1** a fitting out or providing. **2** what one is equipped with; an outfit: *Each player buys his own hockey equipment.* *n.*

es·pe·cial·ly   [es pesh'ə lē]   particularly; principally; chiefly: *This paint is especially designed for use outdoors.* *adv.*

eve·ry·where   [ev'rē wer' *or* ev'rē hwer']   in every place; in all places or lands: *We looked everywhere for our lost kitten.* *adv.*

ex·am·ple   [eg zam'pəl]   **1** a sample; one thing taken to show what the others are like: *Vancouver is an example of a busy city.* **2** a model; pattern of something to be imitated or avoided: *Parents should try to be a good example to their children.* *n.*

ex·cept   [ek sept']   **1** leave out: *No student is excepted from these rules.* **2** other than; apart from; leaving out: *every day except Tuesday.* 1 *v.*, 2 *prep.*

ex·cite   [ek sīt']   **1** stir up the feelings of: *The good news excited everybody.* **2** arouse: *His new jacket excited envy among the other boys.* **3** stir to action: *If you do not excite the animals, they will stay quiet.* *v.*, **ex·cit·ed, ex·cit·ing.**

ex·cit·ed   [ek sī'tid]   stirred up; aroused: *She was so excited about the news that she couldn't sleep.* *adj.*

ex·plode　[ek splōd′]　blow up; burst with a loud noise: *The building was destroyed when the old boiler exploded.* *v.,* **ex·plod·ed, ex·plod·ing.**

ex·plore　[ek splôr′]　**1** go or travel over land, water, or through space, for the purpose of finding out about geographical features, natural resources, etc.: *Champlain explored the Ottawa River and Georgian Bay.* **2** go over carefully; examine: *The children explored the big old house from attic to cellar.* *v.,* **ex·plored, ex·plor·ing.**

F ▼▼▼

fail　[fāl]　fall short of success; not succeed: *She tried hard to win the race, but she failed to do so.* *v.*

fair　[fer]　**1** not favouring one more than the other or others; just; honest: *He is fair even to the people he dislikes.* **2** a gathering of people for the buying and selling of goods, often held at regular times during the year: *a trade fair.* **1** *adj.,* **2** *n.*

fa·mous　[fā′məs]　very well-known; noted: *A great crowd of people greeted the famous hero.* *adj.*

fash·ion·a·ble　[fash′ə nə bəl]　stylish: *fashionable clothes.* *adj.*

fast　[fast]　**1** quick; rapid; swift: *a fast runner.* **2** showing a time ahead of the real time: *That clock is fast.* *adj.*

fa·ther　[fо̄ŦH′ər]　**1** a male parent. **2** a person who is like a father. *n.*

feel·ing　[fē′ling]　the sense of touch: *By feeling, we tell whether a thing is hard or soft.* *n.*

fe·male　[fē′māl]　belonging to the sex that gives birth to young or produces eggs. Mares, cows, and hens are female animals. *adj.*

fence　[fens]　**1** something put around a yard, garden, field, farm, etc. to show where it ends or to keep people or animals out or in: *Most fences are made of wood, wire, or metal.* **2** fight, now only in sport, with long, slender swords called foils. **1** *n.,* **2** *v.,* **fenced, fenc·ing.**

fifth　[fifth]　next after the 4th; last in a series of five; 5th. *adj. or n.*

fight　[fīt]　**1** take part in a violent struggle: *Countries use armies to fight.* **2** a quarrel. **1** *v.,* **fought, fight·ing;** **2** *n.*

film　[film]　a roll or sheet of thin material covered with a special coating and used to take photographs: *She bought two rolls of film for the camera.* *n.*

hat, āge, fär; let, ēqual, tėrm; it, īce; hot, ōpen, ôrder oil, out; cup, pùt, rüle; əbove, takən, pencəl, lemən, circəs ch, child; ng, long; sh, ship th, thin; ŦH, then; zh, measure

fi·nal·ly　[fī′nə lē]　at the end; at last: *The lost dog finally came home.* *adv.*

find　[find]　**1** meet with; come upon: *He found a dollar in the road.* **2** look for and get: *Please find my hat for me.* **3** learn; discover: *We found that he could not swim.* *v.,* **found, find·ing.**

fixed　[fikst]　not movable; firm. *adj.*

flash·light　[flash′līt′]　a portable electric light: *Flashlights are operated by batteries.* *n.*

flight　[flīt]　the act or manner of flying: *the flight of a bird through the air.* *n.*

flow·er　[flou′ər]　**1** a blossom; the part of a plant or tree that produces the seed: *Bees gather nectar from flowers.* **2** produce flowers; bloom; cover with flowers. **1** *n.,* **2** *v.*

fol·low　[fol′ō]　**1** go or come after: *Night follows day.* **2** use; obey; act according to; take as a guide: *Follow her advice.* *v.*

for·ev·er　[fə rev′ər]　without ever coming to an end; for ever. *adv.*

for·ty　[fôr′tē]　four times ten; 40. *n., pl.* **for·ties;** *or adj.*

fought　[fот]　the past tense and past participle of **fight:** *You fought bravely yesterday. A battle was fought there.* *v.*

four　[fôr]　one more than three; 4: *A horse has four legs (adj.).* *n. or adj.* **on all fours,** **a** on all four feet. **b** on hands and knees.

freeze　[frēz]　**1** turn into ice; harden by cold. **2** become suddenly motionless. *v.*

freeze–dry　[frēz′ drī′]　preserve (food, vaccine, etc.) by quick-freezing it and then evaporating the frozen moisture content in a high vacuum. Freeze-dried substances keep for a long period without refrigeration. *v.*

fright·en　[frī′tən]　make afraid. *v.*

front　[frunt]　the forward part: *the front of a car.* *n.*

fur·ni·ture　[fėr′nə chər]　the articles needed in a house or room, such as chairs, tables, beds, desks, etc. *n.*

fur·ry [fėr′ē]   **1** covered with fur: *a furry animal.*
2 soft like fur.   *adj.,* **fur·ri·er, fur·ri·est.**

fu·ture [fyü′chər]   time to come; what is to come:
*You cannot change the past, but you can do better in
the future.   n.*

G ▼▼▼

gait [gāt]   the kind of steps used in going along; a
manner of walking or running: *He has a lame gait
because of an injured foot. A gallop is one of the gaits
of a horse.   n.*

gen·tle [jen′təl]   **1** mild; not severe, rough, or
violent: *a gentle tap.*   **2** soft; low: The cat was purring
with a gentle sound.   **3** kindly; friendly: *a gentle
disposition.   adj.,* **gen·tler, gen·tlest.**

ge·og·ra·phy [jē og′rə fē]   **1** the study of Earth's
surface, climate, continents, countries, peoples,
industries, and products.   **2** the surface features of a
place, region, or country.   *n., pl.* **ge·og·ra·phies.**

glue [glü]   **1** substance used to stick things
together.   **2** fasten with glue.   **3** fasten tightly:
*During the ride down the mountain, her hands were
glued to the steering wheel.*   **1** *n.,* **2, 3** *v.,* **glued,
glu·ing.**

goal [gōl]   **1** the space between two posts into
which, in certain games, a player tries to shoot a puck,
kick a ball, etc. in order to score.   **2** something for
which an effort is made; something wanted; one's aim
or object in doing something: *His goal was to pass his
examinations with high marks.   n.*

goes [gōz]   the present tense form of **go** used
with *he, she, it,* or a singular noun: *She goes to
school.   v.*

gold·en [gōl′dən]   **1** made of or coloured like gold.
2 very good; extremely favourable, valuable, or
important: *golden deeds, a golden opportunity.   adj.*

go·ril·la [gə ril′ə]   the largest and most powerful
ape: *The gorilla is found in the forests of central
Africa.   n.*

grab [grab]   seize suddenly; snatch: *The dog
grabbed the meat and ran.   v.,* **grabbed, grab·bing.**

gra·no·la bar [grə nō′lə bär′]   a snack food in the
shape of a bar, made from a mixture of coarse grains
(granola), often with dried fruit, nuts, honey, etc. in it.

great·ly [grāt′lē]   to a great degree; very much:
*Vaccination greatly reduces the chance of
disease.   adv.*

grid·lock [grid′lok′]   a cessation of activity due
to overloading.   *n.*

grip [grip]   a tight grasp; a firm hold.   *n.,*
gripped, grip·ping.

ground·hog [ground′hog′]   a North American
burrowing animal of the marmot family; woodchuck:
*Groundhogs grow fat in summer and sleep in their
burrows all winter.   n.*

group [grüp]   **1** a number of persons or things
together: *A group of children were playing tag.*
2 bring together; arrange in a group: *He grouped the
tulips in one vase, the roses in another.*   **1** *n.,* **2** *v.*

grow [grō]   become bigger; increase: *Her
business has grown fast.   v.,* **grew, grown, grow·ing.**

guard [gärd]   **1** watch over; take care of; keep
safe: *The dog guards the house.*   **2** a person or group
that guards.   **1** *v.,* **2** *n.*

guide [gīd]   **1** show the way; lead; direct: *The
trapper guided the hunters.*   **2** a person or thing that
shows the way: *Tourists sometimes hire guides.*   **1** *v.,*
guid·ed, guid·ing.   **2** *n.*

guide dog [gīd′ dog′]   a dog specially trained to
guide a blind person; seeing-eye dog.   *n.*

gyros [yē′rō *or* jē′rō *or* jī′rō]   a Greek dish
comprising various meats mixed and cooked on a
vertical skewer which turns in front of heat.   *n.*

H ▼▼▼

hack·er [hak′ər]   **1** one who hacks.   **2** a person
skilled in the use of computers.   *n.*

hair [her]   **1** a fine, threadlike outgrowth from the
skin of human beings and animals.   **2** a mass of such
growths: *A Persian cat has silky hair.   n.*

hand [hand]   **1** the end part of the arm below the
wrist: *Each hand has four fingers and a thumb.*
2 give with the hand; pass: *Please hand me a
spoon.*   **1** *n.,* **2** *v.*

han·dle [han′dəl]   **1** a part of a thing made to be
held or grasped by the hand: *Spoons, pitchers,
hammers, and pails have handles.*   **2** touch, feel, or
use with the hand: *Don't handle that until you buy
it.*   **1** *n.,* **2** *v.,* **han·dled, han·dling.**

hap·pi·ness [hap′ē nis]   **1** the state of being
happy; gladness.   **2** good luck; good fortune.   *n.*

hard·ware [här′dwer′]   **1** articles made from
metal. Locks, hinges, nails, and tools are hardware.
2 the mechanical, electronic, or structural parts of a
computer.   *n.*

have [hav] experience: *Have a pleasant time. They had trouble with this engine.* v., **has, had, hav•ing.**

have•n't [hav'ənt] have not.

ha•zar•dous waste [ha'zər dəs wast'] any material or substance which in normal use can damage the health and well-being of a person. n.

he [ē] a boy, man, or male animal already referred to and identified: *Mike has to work hard, but he likes his job and it pays him well.* pron., pl. **they.**

head [hed] **1** the top part of the human body, where the eyes, ears, nose, and mouth are. **2** at the front or top; leading. 1 n., 2 adj.

heat [hēt] **1** the condition of being hot; hotness; high temperature: *the heat of a fire.* **2** make warm or hot: *The stove heats the room.* 1 n., 2 v.

her•self [hər self'] a form used instead of **she** or **her** when referring back to the subject of the sentence: *She hurt herself.* pron.

hide [hīd] **1** put or keep out of sight; conceal: *Hide where no one else will find it.* **2** hide or conceal oneself: *The gopher hid in its hole.* v., **hid, hid•den** or **hid, hid•ing.**

high•way [hī'wā'] a main road or route: *We took the highway to Edmonton.* n.

hock•ey [hok'ē] a game played on ice by two teams of six players wearing skates and carrying hooked sticks, with which they try to shoot a black rubber disk, the puck, into the opposing team's goal. n.

hold [hōld] grasp and keep: *Hold my watch while I play this game.* v., **held, hold•ing.**

home•less [hōm'lis] **1** having no home. **2 the homeless,** people without homes. adj.

hov•er [huv'ər or hov'ər] **1** stay in or near one place in the air: *The hummingbird hovered in front of the flower.* **2** stay in or near one place; wait nearby: *The children hovered around the kitchen door at mealtime.* v.

huge [hyüj] extremely large or great: *a huge sum of money. An elephant is a huge animal.* adj.

hunt•er [hun'tər] a person who hunts. n.

hus•band [huz'bənd] a married man, especially when thought of in connection with his wife. n.

---

hat, āge, fär; let, ēqual, tėrm; it, īce; hot, ōpen, ôrder
oil, out; cup, pùt, rüle; ə above, takən, pencəl, lemən, circəs
ch, child; ng, long; sh, ship
th, thin; ᴛʜ, then; zh, measure

I

ice•berg [īs'bėrg'] a large mass of ice floating in the sea: *About 90 percent of an iceberg is below the surface of the water.* n.

i•den•ti•fy [i den'tə fī'] recognize as being, or show to be, a particular person or thing; prove to be the same: *He identified the bag as his by telling what it contained.* v., **i•den•ti•fied, i•den•ti•fy•ing.**

in•clude [in klüd'] put in a total, a class, or the like; reckon in a count: *The price includes the land, house, and furniture. All on board the ship were lost, including the captain.* v., **in•clud•ed, in•clud•ing.**

in•for•ma•tion [in'fər mā'shən] knowledge; facts; news: *A dictionary gives information about words.* n.

in•stead [in sted'] in place of someone or something; as a substitute: *She stayed home, and her sister went riding instead.* adv.

in•stru•ment [in'strə mənt] a tool or mechanical device: *a dentist's instruments.* n.

in•ter•est [in'tə rest] **1** a feeling of wanting to know, see, do, own, share in, or take part: *She has an interest in reading and in collecting stamps.* **2** arouse this feeling in: *Art interests me.* 1 n., 2 v.

in•ter•net [in'tər net'] **1 the Internet,** the ensemble of international computer networks. **2** the name of one of these networks: *Are you on Internet or Compuserve?* n.

J

Jan•u•ar•y [jan'yü er'ē] the first month of the year. January has 31 days. n.
☛ *Etymology.* January came into English through Old French from the Latin name for this month, which was based on the name of an ancient god, *Janus,* who had two faces, one looking forward and one looking backward.

jet ski [jet' skē'] **1** a motorized craft for a driver and one or two passengers in single file, with a seat, handlebars, and a ski on the bottom, for skimming over the water. **2** ride or drive such a craft. 1 n. 2 v., **skied, skiing.**

jew•el [jü'əl] a precious stone; gem: *Jewels are worn in necklaces and other ornaments.* n.

jour·ney [jėr′nē] a trip, especially a fairly long one: *a journey around the world.* **2** travel; take a trip: *to journey to New Brunswick.* 1 *n., pl.* **jour·neys.** 2 *v.,* **jour·ney·ed, jour·ney·ing.**

Ju·ly [jə lī′] the seventh month of the year. July has 31 days *n., pl.* **Ju·lies.**
☛ *Etymology.* **July** came into English through Old French from the Latin name for this month. The month was named after Julius Caesar because he was born at this time of the year.

June [jün] the sixth month of the year. June has 30 days. *n.*
☛ *Etymology.* **June** came into English through Old French from the Latin name for this month, *Junonius* or *Junius,* meaning the month of the goddess Juno.

K ▼▼▼

key·board [kē′bôrd′] the set of keys in a piano, typewriter, calculator, computer, etc. *n.*

ki·lo·me·tre [kə lom′ə tər *or* kil′ə mē′tər] a measure of length equal to 1000 metres: *It takes about 10 minutes to walk a kilometre. Symbol:* km *n.*

kind [kīnd] class; sort; variety: *He likes most kinds of candy. A kilt is a kind of skirt. n.*

kind·ness [kīnd′nis] a kind nature; being kind: *We admire her kindness. n., pl.* **kind·ness·es.**

knew [nyü *or* nü] the past tense of **know:** *She knew the right answer. v.*

knives [nīvz] plural of **knife.** *n.*

known [nōn] in the knowledge of everyone; widely recognized: *a known fact, a known artist. adj.*

L ▼▼▼

land [land] come to land; bring to land: *The ship landed at the pier. v.*

large [lärj] of more than the usual size, amount, or number; big: *Canada is a large country. Large crowds come to see our team play. adj.,* **larg·er, larg·est.**

la·ser [lā′zər] a device that produces a very narrow, intense beam of light of only one wavelength and going in only one direction: *Laser beams can cut through metal and are used in surgery, communications, etc. n.*

laugh [laf] **1** make the sounds and the movements of the face and body that show amusement or pleasure at humour or nonsense, etc.: *We all laughed at the joke.* **2** the act or sound of laughing: *a hearty laugh.* 1 *v.,* 2 *n.*

lay [lā] **1** place in a certain position; put down: *Lay your hat on the table.* **2** the past tense of **lie:** *After a long walk I lay down for a rest. v.*

lay·er [lā′ər] one thickness or fold: *the layer of clothing next to the skin. A layer cake is one made of two or more layers put together. n.*

least [lēst] smallest in size, amount, degree, or importance: *Of all our dogs, this one eats the least food. adj.*

lens [lenz] the part of the eye that directs light rays upon the retina. *n., pl.* **lens·es.**

light·ning [līt′ning] a flash of light in the sky caused by a discharge of electricity between clouds, or between a cloud and Earth's surface: *The sound that lightning makes is called thunder. n.*

line [līn] **1** a piece of rope, cord, or wire: *a clothesline, a fish line, a telegraph line.* **2** put a layer of material such as paper, cloth, or felt inside a dress, hat, box, bag, etc. 1 *n.,* 2 *v.*

live [liv] **1** have life; be alive; exist: *All creatures have an equal right to live.* **2** having life; alive: *a live animal.* 1 *v.,* 2 *adj.*

liz·ard [liz′ərd] a reptile with a long body, long tail, movable eyelids, and usually four legs. The iguana, chameleon, and horned toad are lizards. *n.*

load [lōd] **1** what one is carrying; a burden: *The cart has a load of hay. That's a load off my mind!* **2** place on or in a carrier of some kind: *The dockhands are loading grain into the ships.* 1 *n.,* 2 *v.*

lo·cate [lō′kāt *or* lō kāt′] **1** establish in a place: *He located his new store in Yellowknife.* **2** find out the exact position of: *The search party tried to locate the crashed plane. v.,* **lo·cat·ed, lo·cat·ing.**

lock [lok] **1** a means of fastening doors, boxes, etc. usually needing a key of special shape to open it. **2** close with a lock. **3** join, fit, jam, or link together: *They locked arms and walked down the street together.* 1 *n.,* 2, 3 *v.*

log [log] **1** a length of wood just as it comes from the tree. **2** the daily record of a ship's voyage. *n.,* **logged, log·ging.**

logged on [logd on] be able to begin a session of work on a computer by entering a password or other identification. *v.*

long [long]   **1** that measures much from end to end: *A centimetre is short; a kilometre is long.* **2** a long time: *Summer will come before long (n.). Have you been waiting long? (adv.)* **3** wish very much; desire greatly: *He longed for his mother. She longed to see him.* 1 *adj.*, 2 *n. or adv.*, 3 *v.*

loose [lüs]   not firmly set or fastened: *a loose tooth, a loose thread.* *adj.*, **loos•er, loos•est.**

luck [luk]   that which seems to happen or come to one by chance; fortune; chance: *Luck was against the losers, even though they played better.* *n.*

ly•ing [lī′ing]   **1** the telling of a lie; the habit of telling lies. **2** false; not truthful: *a lying report.* **3** the present participle of **lie.** 1 *n.*, 2 *adj.*, 3 *v.*

M ▼▼▼

ma•chine [mə shēn′]   **1** an arrangement of fixed and moving parts for doing work, each part having some special job to do: *The revolving blade of a lawn mower is the part of the machine that cuts the grass.* **2** a device for applying force or changing its direction: *Levers and pulleys are simple machines.* *n.*

main [mān]   **1** most important; largest: *the main dish at dinner, the main street of a town.* **2** a large pipe for water, gas, etc.: *When the water main broke, the street was flooded.* 1 *adj.*, 2 *n.*

make [māk]   **1** bring into being; put together; build; form; shape: *to make a rag rug, to make a boat, to make a medicine.* **2** cause to do or to be: *to make someone happy. She made us work.* *v.*, **made, mak•ing.**

male [māl]   **1** a man, boy, or male animal: *All fathers are males.* **2** belonging to the sex that can father young: *Bulls and stallions are male animals.* 1 *n.*, 2 *adj.*
☛ *Homonyms.* **Male** is pronounced like **mail.**

mam•mal [mam′əl]   any of the class of warm-blooded animals that have a backbone, and the females of which have glands that produce milk for feeding their young. Human beings, cattle, dogs, cats, and whales are all mammals. *n.*

Man•i•to•ban [man′ə tō′bən]   **1** a person born in or living in Manitoba. **2** of or having to do with Manitoba. 1 *n.*, 2 *adj.*

map [map]   **1** make a map of; show on a map. **2** plan; arrange in detail: *Each Monday we mapped out the week's work.* *v.*, **mapped, map•ping.**
☛ *Usage.* **Map** may refer especially to a plan of roads or other routes on land, while **chart** is used especially for plans showing air or sea routes. An **atlas** is a book of maps covering a large area or the whole world.

hat, āge, fär; let, ēqual, tėrm; it, īce; hot, ōpen, ôrder
oil, out; cup, pùt, rüle; əbove, takən, pencəl, lemən, circəs
ch, child; ng, long; sh, ship
th, thin; ᴛʜ, then; zh, measure

mar•ry [mar′ē *or* mer′ē]   **1** join as husband and wife: *The minister married them.* **2** take as husband or wife: *John planned to marry Angela.* *v.*, **mar•ried, mar•ry•ing.**

match [mach]   **1** a short, slender piece of wood or pasteboard, tipped with a mixture that takes fire when rubbed on a rough or specially prepared surface. **2** be equal to in a contest: *No one could match the skill of the unknown archer.* **3** be alike; go well together: *The rugs and the drapes match.* 1 *n.*, 2, 3 *v.*

means [mēnz]   **1** the method or methods by which something is made to happen or brought about: *The airplane is a fast means of travel. We won the game by fair means.* **2** riches; wealth: *He is a man of means. A woman of means.* *n.*

med•i•cal [med′ə kəl]   having to do with healing or with the science and art of medicine: *medical advice, medical schools, medical supplies.* *adj.*

melt [melt]   change from solid to liquid by the action of heat: *Ice becomes water when it melts. Great heat melts iron.* *v.*

men•u [men′yü]   in computer programs, a list of choices that allows the user to select a topic. *n.*

met•al [met′əl]   a substance that is usually shiny, a good conductor of heat and electricity, and can be made into wire, or hammered into sheets. Gold, silver, copper, iron, lead, tin, and aluminum are metals. *n.*

Mex•i•can [mek′sə kən]   **1** a person born in or living in Mexico. **2** of or having to do with Mexico or its people. 1 *n.*, 2 *adj.*

mi•cro•chip [mī′krō chip′]   a very small piece of semiconducting material containing the information for a computer circuit. *n.*

mi•cro•scope [mī′krə skōp′]   an instrument with a lens or combination of lenses for making small objects look larger so that one can see things not visible to the naked eye. *n.*

mid•dle [mid′əl]   halfway between; in the centre; at the same distance from either end or side: *the middle house in the row.* *adj.*

mil•lion [mil′yən]   **1** one thousand thousand (1 000 000). **2** a very large number; very many: *She claims to have millions of dollars (n.).* *n. or adj.*

min·ute¹ [min′it] **1** one of the 60 equal periods of time that make up an hour; 60 seconds. *Symbol*: min **2** a short time; an instant: *I'll be there in a minute.* *n.*

mi·nute² [mī nyüt′ *or* mī nüt′] **1** very small; tiny: *a minute speck of dust.* **2** going into or concerned with small details: *She gave me minute instructions about how to do my work.* *adj.*

miss·ing [mis′ing] **1** out of its usual place: *The missing ring was found under the dresser. One of the books was missing.* **2** absent: *Four children were missing from class today.* *adj.*

mo·dem [mō′ dem′] a device which enables a computer to receive and send data over telephone lines. *n.*

mod·ern [mod′ərn] of the present time; of times not long past: *Colour television is a modern invention.* *adj.*

Mon·day [mun′dā′ *or* mun′dē] the second day of the week, the day after Sunday. *n.*
☛ *Etymology.* **Monday** developed from Old English *monandæg*, meaning 'day of the moon'.

mon·o·rail [mon′ə rāl] **1** a single rail serving as a complete track for a wheeled vehicle. **2** a railway in which cars run on a single track. *n.*

month [munth] one of the twelve periods of time into which a year is divided. *n.*

mo·tor [mō′tər] **1** an engine that makes a machine go: *an electric motor, a gasoline motor.* **2** causing or having to do with motion: *Motor nerves arouse muscles to action.* 1 *n.*, 2 *adj.*

moun·tain [moun′tən] a very high hill: *the Rocky Mountains.* *n.*

mouse [mous] **1** a small rodent native to the Old World but now common throughout North America, having a pointed snout, large ears, and a long, scaly tail. **2** a hand-held input device for a computer that controls the location of an object or a cursor on a screen and allows commands to be entered. *n.*

move·ment [müv′mənt] **1** the act of moving. **2** a program by a group of people to bring about something: *the movement for peace.* *n.*

mus·cle [mus′əl] **1** the tissue in the bodies of people and animals that can be tightened or loosened so as to make the body move. **2** strength. *n.*

mus·ic vi·de·o [myü′ zik vid′ē ō′] a short videotape featuring a piece of music such as a rock song. *n.*

N ▼▼▼

nat·u·ral [nach′ə rəl] produced by nature; coming or occurring in the ordinary course of events: *natural feelings, natural curls, a natural complexion, a natural death, a natural result.* *adj.*

noise [noiz] **1** a sound that is not musical or pleasant; loud or harsh sound: *The noise kept me awake.* **2** any sound: *the noise of rain on the roof.* *n.*

north [nôrth] the direction to which a compass needle points; the direction to the right as one faces the setting sun. *n.*

no·tice [nō′tis] **1** see; take note of; give attention to: *I noticed that my purse was gone.* **2** a written or printed sign; a paper posted in a public place; a large sheet of paper giving information or directions: *We saw a notice of this week's movie outside the theatre.* 1 *v.*, 2 *n.*

No·vem·ber [nō vem′bər] the eleventh month of the year; the month before December. November has 30 days. *n.*
☛ *Etymology.* **November** came into English through Old French from the Latin name for this month, *November*, from *novem*, meaning 'nine'. November was the ninth month of the ancient Roman calendar.

O ▼▼▼

ob·ject [ob′jikt *for 1*, əb jekt′ *for 2*] **1** anything that can be seen or touched: *What is that object by the fence?* **2** make objections; be opposed; feel dislike: *Many people object to loud noise.* 1 *n.*, 2 *v.*

of·fen·sive [ə fen′siv] **1** giving offence; irritating; annoying: *'Shut up' is an offensive remark.* **2** a position or attitude of attack: *The army took the offensive.* 1 *adj.*, 2 *n.*

of·fi·cer [of′ə sər] a person who commands others in the armed forces, such as a colonel, a lieutenant, or a captain. *n.*

of·ten [of′ən *or* of′tən] many times; frequently: *It snows often in the mountains.* *adv.*

oil [oil] **1** petroleum. **2** a fatty or greasy substance made in the bodies of plants and animals. **3** put oil on or in: *The technician oiled the wheels.* 1, 2 *n.*, 3 *v.*

old [ōld] **1** not young; having been or existed for some time; aged: *an old wall surrounds the castle. We are old friends.* **2** the time of long ago; the past: *the heroes of old.* 1 *adj.*, 2 *n.* **old·er** or **eld·er, old·er** or **eld·est.**

O·lym·pic games [ō lim′pik gāmz′] **1** contests in athletics, poetry, and music, held every four years by the ancient Greeks. **2** modern athletic contests held every four years in a different country: *Athletes from many nations compete in the Olympic games.*

or·der [ôr′dər] the way one thing follows another: *in order of size, in alphabetical order, to copy them in order. n.*

or·gan·ize [ôr′gə nīz′] **1** arrange to work or come together as a whole: *The general organized his soldiers into a powerful fighting force.* **2** arrange in a system: *She organized her thoughts. He organized his stamp collection. v.,* **or·gan·ized, or·gan·iz·ing.**

out·doors [out′dôrz′] **1** out in the open air; not indoors: *Mom won't let us go outdoors until it stops raining.* **2** the world outside of buildings; the open air. **1** *adv.,* **2** *n.*

ox·y·gen [ok′sə jən] a gas without colour or odour that forms about one fifth of the air. Animals and plants cannot live without oxygen. *n.*

o·zone lay·er [ō′zōn lā′ər] a layer in Earth's atmosphere about 15 to 30 km above the earth, that contains a lot of ozone. It absorbs much of the sun's ultraviolet radiation and keeps much of Earth's warmth from escaping.

P

paint·er¹ [pān′tər] **1** a person who paints pictures; artist. **2** a person who paints houses, woodwork, etc. *n.*

pair [per] **1** a single thing consisting of two parts that cannot be used separately: *a pair of scissors, a pair of pants.* **2** a set of two separate but matching things: *a pair of socks. n.*

pants [pants] an outer garment for the lower part of the body, reaching from the waist to the ankles and divided to cover each leg separately; trousers. *n.*

pass [pas] **1** go by; move past: *The parade passed. We passed the big truck. Many people pass our house every day.* **2** go from one to another: *The property passed from my grandmother to my parents.* **3** get through or by: *The ship passed the channel.* **4** be successful in (an examination or course): *We all passed arithmetic.* **5** a free ticket: *a pass to the circus.* **6** a narrow road, path, channel, etc.: *A pass crosses the mountains.* **1–4** *v.,* **passed, pass·ing. 5, 6** *n.*

pause [poz] a moment of silence; a brief stop; a rest: *He made a short pause and then went on reading. n.,* **paused, paus·ing.**

paw [po] **1** the foot of a four-footed animal having claws. Cats and dogs have paws. **2** *Informal.* handle awkwardly or rudely: *The customers pawed the shirts on the bargain counter.* **1** *n.,* **2** *v.*

ped·al [ped′əl] **1** a lever worked by the foot; the part on which the foot is placed to move any kind of machinery. **2** work something by pushing such a lever with the foot: *to pedal a bike.* **1** *n.,* **2** *v.,* **ped·alled** or **ped·aled, ped·al·ling** or **ped·al·ing.**

peo·ple [pē′pəl] men, women, and children; persons: *There were ten people present. n.,* **peo·pled, peo·pling.**

per·haps [pər haps′] maybe; it may be; possibly: *Perhaps a letter will come today. adv.*

pho·to·graph [fō′tə graf′] **1** a picture made with a camera. A photograph is made by the action of light rays from the thing pictured, coming through the lens of the camera onto a piece of film. **2** take a photograph of. **1** *n.,* **1** *v.*

pho·tog·ra·phy [fə tog′rə fē] the taking of photographs. *n.*

pic·ture [pik′chər] **1** a drawing, painting, portrait, or photograph; a printed copy of any of these. **2** a mental image; idea: *I have a clear picture of the problem. n.,* **pic·tured, pic·tur·ing.**

piece [pēs] **1** one of the parts into which a thing is divided or broken; a bit: *The cup broke in pieces.* **2** a portion; limited part; small quantity: *a piece of land containing one hectare, a piece of bread. n.,* **pieced, piec·ing.**

pi·lot [pī′lət] **1** a person who operates the controls of an aircraft in flight. **2** act as a pilot of; steer: *This businessman pilots his own airplane.* **1** *n.,* **2** *v.*

pi·o·neer [pī′ə nēr′] **1** a person who settles in a region that has not been settled before. **2** prepare or open up for others; take the lead: *Astronauts are pioneering in exploring outer space.* **1** *n.,* **2** *v.*

pi·ta [pē′tə] a Mediterranean form of round, flat bread having a pocket which can be stuffed with meat, vegetables, etc. *n.*

plain [plān] a flat stretch of land; prairie: *the western plains. Cattle wandered over the plain. n.* ☛ *Homonyms.* **Plain** is pronounced like **plane.**

plane [plān] **1** a flat or level surface. **2** an airplane. **3** a carpenter's tool with a blade for smoothing or shaping wood. *n.*

plan·et [plan′it] one of the heavenly bodies that move around the sun in regular paths. Mercury, Venus, Earth, Mars, Jupiter, Saturn, Uranus, Neptune, and Pluto are planets. *n.*

play·er [plā′ər] 1 a person who plays: *a baseball player, a card player.* 2 a device that plays: *a record player. n.*

point [point] 1 a unit of scoring or measuring: *Four points win a game in tennis.* 2 direct a finger, weapon, etc.; aim: *Don't point your finger at me.* 1 *n.,* 2 *v.*

pol·lu·tion [pə lü′shən] polluting or being polluted. *n.*

port [pôrt] 1 a harbour; a place where ships and boats can take shelter from storms or unload cargo. 2 a receptacle on a computer to which a communication cable can be connected. *n.*

pos·si·ble [pos′ə bəl] that can be; that can be done; that can happen: *Come if possible. It is possible to cure tuberculosis. adj.*

prac·tice [prak′tis] the doing of something many times over in order to gain skill: *Practice makes perfect. n.*

pre·his·tor·ic [prē′his tô′rik] of or belonging to time before histories were written: *Fossils and stone tools give us information about prehistoric people and animals. adj.*

prob·a·bly [prob′ə blē] more likely than not. *adv.*

prob·lem [prob′ləm] 1 matter or cause of doubt or difficulty: *Starvation is a major problem in many countries.* 2 something to be worked out: *a problem in arithmetic. n.*

pro·gram or **pro·gramme** [prō′gram] 1 a printed list of items or events; a list of performers, players, etc.: *a concert program, a theatre program, a hockey program.* 2 prepare a set of instructions for a computer so that it may perform some specific operation. 1 *n.,* 2 *v.,* **programmed, programming.**

prom·ise [prom′is] 1 the words that bind a person to do or not to do something: *A person of honour always keeps a promise.* 2 an indication of what may be expected: *The clouds give promise to rain. n.,* **prom·ised, prom·is·ing.**

purr [pėr] a low, murmuring sound such as a cat makes when pleased. *n.*

pyr·a·mid [pir′ə mid′] 1 a solid form having triangular sides that meet at a point. 2 **the Pyramids,** pl. the huge, massive stone pyramids, serving as royal tombs, built by the ancient Egyptians. *n.*

Q ▼▼▼

quar·ter [kwô′tər] one of four equal parts; half of a half; one fourth: *a quarter of an apple, a quarter of lamb. A quarter of an hour is 15 minutes. n.*

quick [kwik] 1 fast and sudden; swift: *The cat made a quick jump. Many weeds have a quick growth.* 2 coming soon; prompt: *a quick reply. adj.*

qui·et [kwī′ət] making no sound; with little or no noise: *quiet footsteps, a quiet room. adj.*

quit [kwit] 1 stop: *The women quit work at five. It will soon be time to quit.* 2 rid; free; clear: *I gave him money to be quit of him.* 1 *v.,* **quit** or **quit·ted, quit·ting;** 2 *adj.*

R ▼▼▼

ra·di·o [rā′dē ō′] the sending and receiving of electromagnetic waves to carry music, messages, or information between distant points without wires: *We can listen to music broadcast by radio. n., pl.* **ra·di·os,** *v.,* **ra·di·oed, ra·di·o·ing.**

ranch [ranch] 1 a large farm with grazing land, used for raising cattle, sheep, or horses. 2 any farm, especially one used to raise one kind of animal or crop: *a fruit ranch, a chicken ranch. n.*

reach [rēch] 1 get to; arrive at; come to: *Your letter reached me yesterday.* 2 range; power; capacity: *Philosophy is beyond the reach of children; they cannot understand it.* 1 *v.,* 2 *n.*

rea·son [rē′zən] 1 a cause or motive for an action, feeling, etc.: *Tell me your reasons for not liking him.* 2 an explanation: *Sickness is the reason for her absence. n.*
☞ *Usage.* **Reason** and **cause** often mean the same, but they must not be confused. A **reason** explains why or how something happens: *His reason for being late was that his car would not start.* A **cause** is what makes something happen: *The extreme cold was the cause of his car not starting.*

re·ceive [ri sēv′] 1 take something sent or offered: *We receive many presents at Christmas.* 2 be given; get: *The soldier received a letter from home. v.,* **re·ceived, re·ceiv·ing.**

rec·tan·gle [rek′tang′gəl] a four-sided figure with four right angles. *n.*

re·duce [ri dyüs′ *or* ri düs′] make less; make smaller; decrease: *We have reduced expenses this year. v.,* **re·duced, re·duc·ing.**

re·main [ri mān′] 1 continue in a place; stay: *We shall remain at the lake till September.* 2 **remains,** *pl.* **a** what is left: *The remains of the meal were fed to the dog.* **b** a dead body: *His remains were lowered into the grave.* 1 *v.,* 2 *n.*

re·mark·a·ble [ri mär′kə bəl] worthy of notice; unusual: *a remarkable memory*. *adj.*

re·mem·ber [ri mem′ber] **1** call back to mind: *I can't remember that man's name*. **2** keep in mind as deserving a reward, gift, etc.; make a gift to: *My uncle remembered us in his will*. *v.*

re·ply [ri plī′] respond or answer: *She replied that she was tired*. *v.*, **re·plied, re·ply·ing.**

re·turn [ri tėrn′] **1** go back; come back: *Your mother will return in a moment*. **2** a profit; an amount received: *The returns from the sale were more than a hundred dollars*. **1** *v.*, **2** *n.*

re·ward [ri wôrd′] a return made for something done. *n.*

ride [rīd] **1** sit on a horse and make it go. **2** be carried along by anything: *to ride on a train, to ride in a car*. **3** move or float on the water: *The ship rides at anchor*. **4** a trip on horseback, in an automobile, on a train, etc. **1** **3** *v.*, **rode, rid·den, rid·ing;** **4** *n.*

right [rīt] **1** that which is right, just, good, true: *Do right, not wrong*. **2** correctly; truly: *I guessed right*. **3** fitting; suitable; proper: *Learn to say the right thing at the right time*. **1** *n.*, **2** *adv.*, **3** *adj.*

ro·bot [rō′bot] any machine that works automatically or by remote control, especially one that performs human tasks or has the appearance of a human being. *n.*

ro·bo·tics [rō bot′ iks] the development and use of robots to perform tasks normally done by people. *n.*

rol·ler·blad·ing [rō lər blā′ ding] a kind of roller skating using skates (roller blades) that have four narrow wheels in a single row down the centre of the skate. *v.*

rule [rüle] **1** a statement of what to do and what not to do; a principle governing conduct, action, etc.: *Obey the rules of the game*. **2** make a rule; decide: *The judge ruled against them*. **1** *n.*, **2** *v.*

S ▼▼▼

scan [skan] look closely, examine with care *Electronics*. pass a rapidly moving beam of light over in order to sense and transmit or reproduce an image of it as for television or input to a computer. *v.*

scar·y [sker′ē] *Informal.* causing fright or alarm: *She tells scary stories on Halloween*. *adj.*

---

hat, āge, fär; let, ēqual, tėrm; it, īce; hot, ōpen, ôrder oil, out; cup, pùt, rüle; əbove, takən, pencəl, lemən, circəs ch, child; ng, long; sh, ship th, thin; ŦH, then; zh, measure

---

scene [sēn] a view; picture: *The white sailboats in the blue water made a pretty scene*.
☛ *Homonyms.* **Scene** is pronounced like **seen.**
☛ *Etymology.* **Scene** comes from a Greek word *skēnē*, which originally meant the tent where actors changed their costumes.

sci·ence [sī′əns] knowledge based on observed facts and tested truths arranged in an orderly system: *the laws of science*. *n.*

score [skôr] **1** the record of points made in a game, contest, or test: *The score was 9 to 2 in favour of our school*. **2** make points or a gain; succeed: *She had difficulty getting a job but scored at last*. **1** *n.*, **2** *v.*

scrolled [skrōld] *Computer.* move the lines of writing on the screen of a computer's video display up or down to allow room for a new line to be added. *v.*

search [sėrch] try to find by looking; seek; look for: *We searched all day for the lost kitten*. *v.*

seat [sēt] **1** something to sit on: *Chairs, benches, and stools are seats*. **2** a place in a parliament, a city council, etc.: *The candidate lost his seat in the last election*. *n.*

seem [sēm] appear; appear to be: *This apple seemed good but was rotten inside*. *v.*

send [send] drive; throw: *to send a ball*. *The volcano sent clouds of smoke into the air*. *v.*, **sent, send·ing.**

serve [sėrv] work for; be a servant for: *Slaves are forced to serve their masters. Good citizens serve their country*. *v.*, **served, serv·ing.**

shoot [shüt] **1** send with force or speed at a target: *He shot the puck into the open net*. **2** a new part growing out; a young branch: *See the new shoots on that bush*. **1** *v.*, **shot, shoot·ing;** **2** *n.*

shore [shôr] the land at the edge of a sea, lake, etc.: *They walked along the shore*. *n.*

should [shùd; *unstressed*, shəd] the past tense of **shall**, used: **1** to mean that one ought to do something: *Everyone should learn to swim. I really should do my homework before I go out*. **2** to suggest that the speaker is uncertain about a thing or unwilling to believe something: *I don't see why you should think that. It's strange that they should be so late*. *v.*

sign [sīn] **1** give a sign to; signal: *The guard signed the visitor to enter.* **2** an indication; trace; evidence: *There were no signs of life about the house. The robin is a sign of spring.* **1** *v.,* **2** *n.*

sig·nal [sig′nəl] **1** a sign giving notice of something: *A red light is a signal of danger.* **2** make a signal or signals to: *He signalled the car to stop by raising his hand.* **3** remarkable; striking: *The airplane was a signal invention.* **1** *n.,* **2** *v.,* **sig·nalled** or **sig·naled, sig·nal·ling** or **sig·nal·ing;** **3** *adj.*

si·lent [sī′lənt] **1** quiet; still; noiseless: *a silent house.* **2** not speaking; saying little or nothing: *The stranger was silent about his early life. Students must be silent during the study hour.* *adj.*

since [sins] **1** from a past time till now: *We have been up since five.* **2** before now; ago: *Old Rover died long since.* **3** because: *Since you feel tired, you should rest.* **1** *prep.,* **2** *adv.,* **3** *conj.*

size [sīz] **1** the amount of surface or space a thing takes up: *The two boys are of the same size.* **2** arrange according to size: *Size these nails.* **1** *n.,* **2** *v.*

skate·board [skāt′bôrd′] a small, narrow board of wood or plastic, usually about 45–50 cm long, shaped somewhat like a surfboard, but equipped with a pair of roller-skate wheels at each end and used for coasting along streets, sidewalks, etc. *n.*

skill [skil] ability gained by practice or knowledge; expertness: *It takes skill to tune a piano.* *n.*

skull [skull] the bones of the head; the part of the skeleton that encloses and protects the brain. *n.*

slip [slip] **1** go or move smoothly, quietly, easily or quickly: *She slipped out of the room. Time slips by. The ship slips through the waves.* **2** pass without notice; pass through neglect; escape: *Don't let this opportunity slip.* **3** a narrow strip of paper, wood, etc. **1, 2** *v.,* **slipped, slip·ping,** **3** *n.*

slow [slō] taking a long time; taking longer than usual; not fast or quick: *a slow journey.* *adj.*

smoke [smōk] the mixture of gases and carbon that can be seen rising in a cloud from anything burning. *n.,* **smoked, smok·ing.**

sol·id [sol′id] **1** not a liquid or a gas: *Water becomes solid when it freezes.* **2** not hollow: *A bar of iron is solid; a pipe is hollow.* **3** strongly made or put together: *This is not a very solid table.* **4** *Geometry,* a figure that has length, breadth, and thickness: *A cube is a solid.* **1–3** *adj.,* **4** *n.*

some·one [sum′wun′] some person; somebody: *Someone has to lock up the house.* *pron.*

south [south] the direction to the left as one faces the setting sun; the direction opposite to north. *n.*

south·ern [suTH′ərn] **1** toward the south: *a southern view.* **2** from the south: *a southern breeze.* **3** of or in the south: *He has travelled in southern countries.* *adj.*

space ship or **space·ship** [spās′ship′] a vehicle designed for travel between the planets or in outer space. *n.*

speak·er·phone [spē′ kər fōn′] a telephone equipped with a microphone and loudspeaker, so that no handpiece is needed and more than one person can participate in the call. *n.*

spe·cial [spesh′əl] **1** of a particular kind; distinct from others; not general: *This bicycle has a special frame. Have you any special colour in mind for your new coat?* **2** a product especially featured in a store; bargain: *a weekend special on stereos.* **1** *adj.,* **2** *n.*

speed [spēd] **1** swift or rapid movement. **2** go faster than is safe or lawful: *The car was caught speeding near the school zone.* **1** *n.,* **2** *v.,* **sped** or **speed·ed, speed·ing.**

spike [spīk] **1** a large, strong nail. **2** fasten with spikes: *The men spiked the rails to the ties when laying the track.* **3** a sharp-pointed piece or part: *The baseball players wore shoes with spikes.* **1, 3** *n.,* **2** *v.,* **spiked, spik·ing.**

spi·ral [spī′rəl] **1** a winding and gradually widening coil: *The spring of a watch is a spiral.* **2** move in a spiral: *The flaming airplane spiralled to Earth.* **1** *n.,* **2** *v.,* **spi·ralled, spi·ral·ling.**

spokes·per·son [spōks′ pėr′ sən] a person who speaks for another or others. *n.*

spook·y [spü′kē] like or suggesting spooks; weird; scary. *adj.*

sport [spôrt] a game, contest, or other pastime requiring some skill and a certain amount of exercise. *n.*

sports·plex [spôrts′ pleks′] a multipurpose recreational site providing facilities for a number of indoor and outdoor sports, such as swimming, tennis, skating, at the same time. *n.*

spot [spot] **1** a mark, stain, or speck: *You have grease spots on your suit.* **2** *Informal.* pick out; find out; recognize: *I spotted my sister in the crowd. The teacher spotted every mistake in my paper.* **1** *n.,* **2** *v.,* **spot·ted, spot·ting.**

stalk [stok] **1** the main stem of a plant. **2** approach or pursue without being seen or heard: *The cougar stalked the deer.* **1** *n.,* **2** *v.*

start [stärt] **1** begin to move, go, or act: *The train started on time.* **2** a sudden movement; jerk: *On seeing the snake, the man sprang up with a start. I awoke with a start.* 1 *v.*, 2 *n.*

state [stāt] **1** the condition of a person or thing: *He is in a state of poor health.* **2** the physical condition of a material with regard to its structure, composition, or form: *Ice is water in a solid state.* **3** tell in speech or writing; express; say: *State your opinion of the new school rules.* 1, 2 *n.*, 3 *v.*, **stat•ed, stat•ing.**

sta•tion [stā'shən] a place to stand in; a place that a person is appointed to occupy in the performance of some duty: *The police officer took her station at the corner.* *n.*

stay [stā] **1** remain; continue to be: *Stay still.* **2** a strong rope, chain, or wire attached to something to steady it: *The mast of a ship is held in place by stays.* 1 *v.*, 2 *n.*

step [step] a movement made by lifting the foot and putting it down again in a new position; one motion of the leg in walking, running, dancing, etc. *n.*

stock [stok] **1** cattle or other farm animals; livestock: *The farm was sold with all its stock.* **2** lay in a supply of; supply: *Our camp is well stocked with everything we need for a short stay.* 1 *n.*, 2 *v.*

stood [stud] the past tense and past participle of **stand**: *He stood in the corner for five minutes. This building has stood here for many years.* *v.*

straight [strāt] **1** without a bend or curve: *a straight line, a straight path, straight hair.* **2** frankly; honestly; uprightly: *Talk straight.* 1 *adj.*, 2 *adv.*
☛ *Homonyms.* **Straight** is pronounced like **strait.**

strange [strānj] **1** unusual; queer; peculiar: *What a strange experience!* **2** not known, seen, or heard of before; not familiar: *She is moving to a strange place.* *adj.*

strong [strong] **1** having much force or power: *A strong person can lift heavy things.* **2** able to last, endure, resist, etc.: *a strong fort, a strong rope.* *adj.*

style [stīl] **1** fashion: *He dresses in the latest style. Her clothes are out of style.* **2** a manner; method; way: *She learned several styles of swimming.* *n.*

suc•cess [sək ses'] a favourable result; a wished-for ending; good fortune: *Success in school comes from intelligence and work.* *n.*

sud•den [sud'ən] **1** not expected: *a sudden attack.* **2** quick; rapid: *The cat made a sudden jump at the mouse.* *adj.*

---

hat, āge, fär; let, ēqual, tėrm; it, īce; hot, ōpen, ôrder
oil, out; cup, pùt, rüle; əbove, takən, pencəl, lemən, circəs
ch, child; ng, long; sh, ship
th, thin; ᴛʜ, then; zh, measure

---

suit [süt] **1** a set of clothes to be worn together: *A man's suit consists of a coat and pants, and sometimes, a vest.* **2** be good for; agree with: *A cold climate suits apples and wheat, but not oranges and tea.* 1 *n.*, 2 *v.*

sun•block [sun' blok'] a powerful sunscreen that offers a degree of protection against sun by blocking out all or nearly all of the harmful ultraviolet rays. *n.*

sup•port [sə pôrt'] **1** keep from falling; hold up: *Walls support the roof.* **2** give strength or courage to; keep up; help: *Hope supports us in trouble.* **3** provide for: *She supports a family of five.* **4** a person or thing that supports; a prop: *She had to wear a neck support after the accident.* 1–3 *v.*, 4 *n.*

sup•er mo•del [sü' pər mo'dəl] a model who has become a star. *n.*

su•preme [sə prēm'] highest in rank or authority: *a supreme ruler, a supreme court.* *adj.*

sur•face [sėr'fis] **1** the outside of anything: *An egg has a smooth surface.* **2** the top of the ground, or of a body of water or other liquid: *The miners returned to the surface.* **3** the outward appearance: *He seems rough, but you will find him very kind below the surface.* *n.*

sur•prise [sər prīz'] **1** a feeling caused by something unexpected. *His face showed surprise at the news.* **2** something causing this feeling: *Her visit was a surprise.* **3** cause to feel surprised; astonish: *The results of the race surprised us.* 1, 2 *n.*, 3 *v.*, **sur•prised, sur•pris•ing.**

swift [swift] **1** moving very fast; able to move very fast: *a swift canoe.* **2** coming or happening quickly: *a swift answer.* *adj.*

T ▼▼▼

talk•ing book [tok'ing bùk'] a book made into an audio recording by being read onto a cassette tape or a series of cassette tapes. *n.*

tak•en [tā'kən] the past participle of **take**: *I have taken this toy from the shelf.* *v.*
taken aback, suddenly surprised or startled.

teach•er [tē'chər] a person who teaches, especially one who teaches in a school. *n.*

tel·e·scope [tel′ə skōp′] **1** an instrument for making distant objects appear nearer and larger: *The stars are studied by means of telescopes.* **2** force or be forced together, one inside another, like the sliding tubes of some telescopes: *When the two railway trains crashed into each other, the cars were telescoped.* **1** *n.,* **2** *v.,* **tel·e·scoped, tel·e·scop·ing.**

tem·per·a·ture [tem′pə rə chər] the degree of heat or cold: *The temperature of freezing water is 0 degrees Celsius.* *n.*

ter·ri·ble [ter′ə bəl] **1** causing great fear; terrible; awful: *The terrible storm destroyed many lives.* **2** extremely bad; unpleasant: *She has a terrible temper.* *adj.*

thank·ful [thangk′fəl] feeling thanks; grateful: *He is thankful for good health.* *adj.*

their [THer] a possessive form of **they**: of them; belonging to them: *They did their best. They all raised their hands. That's their house.* *adj.*
☛ *Homonyms.* **Their** is pronounced like **there** and **they're.**
☛ *Usage.* **Their, theirs** are the possessive forms of **they. Their** is always followed by a noun: *This is their farm.* **Theirs** stands alone: *This farm is theirs.*

there [THer] **1** in that place; at that place; at that point: *Sit there. Finish reading the page and stop there.* **2** in that matter: *You are mistaken there.* *adv.*

they'd [THād] **1** they had. **2** they would.

they're [THer] they are.
☛ *Homonyms.* **They're** is pronounced like **their** and **there.**

thief [thēf] a person who steals, especially one who steals secretly and, usually, without using force: *A thief stole the bicycle from the yard.* *n., pl.* **thieves.**

though [THō] **1** in spite of the fact that: *We take our medicine, though we do not like it. Though it was pouring, they went swimming.* **2** however; nevertheless: *I am sorry for our quarrel; you began it, though.* **1** *conj.,* **2** *adv.*

thought [thot] **1** what a person thinks; an idea or notion: *Her thought was to have a picnic.* **2** the past tense and past participle of **think**: *We thought it would snow yesterday.* **1** *n.,* **2** *v.*

through [thrü] **1** from end to end of; from side to side of; between the parts of: *He had a job through the summer.* **2** having reached the end; finished: *I will soon be through.* **1** *prep.,* **2** *adj.*

throw [thrō] cast; toss; hurl: *The catcher threw the ball. The fire hose threw water on the burning house.* *v.,* **threw, thrown, throw·ing.**

thumb [thum] **1** the short, thick finger of the hand. **2** leaf through or turn the pages of a book or magazine rapidly: *She thumbed through the book and gave it back to me.* **1** *n.,* **2** *v.*

Thurs·day [thėrz′dā′ or thėrz′dē] the fifth day of the week, following Wednesday. *n.*
☛ *Etymology.* **Thursday** developed from Old English *Thunresdæg,* originally meaning 'day of Thor'; Thor was the Germanic god of thunder.

ti·ny [tī′nē] very small; wee: *a tiny baby chicken.* *adj.* **ti·ni·er, ti·ni·est.**

to·fu [tō′ fü] a bland, protein-rich food of a cheeselike consistency, made from soybeans. It is a popular meat substitute. *n.*

to·ward [tə wôrd′] in the direction of: *He walked toward the north.* *prep.*

track [trak] follow by means of footprints, marks, smell, etc. *v.*

traf·fic [traf′ik] **1** the people, automobiles, wagons, ships, etc. coming and going along a way of travel. **2** carry on trade; buy; sell; exchange. **1** *n.,* **2** *v.,* **traf·ficked, traf·fick·ing.**

trail [trāl] **1** a path across a wild or unsettled region: *The prospector had followed mountain trails for days.* **2** follow along behind; follow: *The dog trailed its master constantly.* **1** *n.,* **2** *v.*

trail bike [trāl bīk] a small motorcycle for riding on rough terrain. *n.*

trail mix [trāl′ miks′] a high-energy snack food made of a mixture of nuts, dried fruit, sunflower seeds, etc. *n.*

train·ing [trā′ning] **1** practical education in some art, profession, etc.: *training for teachers.* **2** a good condition maintained by exercise and care: *The athlete was advised to keep in training.* *n.*

trav·el [trav′əl] **1** go from one place to another: *She is travelling in Europe this summer.* **2** move; proceed; pass: *Sound travels in waves.* *v.,* **trav·elled** or **trav·eled, trav·el·ling** or **trav·el·ing.**

treas·ure [trezh′ər] **1** wealth or riches stored up; valuable things: *The pirates buried treasure along the coast.* **2** value highly: *She treasures that doll more than all her other toys.* **1** *n.,* **2** *v.,* **treas·ured, treas·ur·ing.**

trick [trik] **1** a clever act; a feat of skill: *We enjoyed the tricks of the trained animals.* **2** something done to get the better of a person by deceiving him or her. **3** get the better of by deceiving. 1, 2 *n.*, 3 *v.*

tro·phy [trō'fē] a prize, cup, etc. awarded to a victorious person or team: *She kept her tennis trophy on the mantelpiece. n., pl.* **tro·phies.**

tur·tle [tėr'təl] an animal having a body enclosed in a hard shell into which it can draw its head and legs. Turtles live in fresh water, in salt water, or on land; those living on land are often called tortoises. *n.*

twen·ty-five [twen'tē fīv'] two times ten plus five. *n. or adj.*

twice [twīs] **1** two times: *Twice two is four.* **2** doubly: *twice as much. adv.*

U

un·der·stand [un'dər stand'] get the meaning of; comprehend: *Now I understand the teacher's question. v.,* **un·der·stood, un·der·stand·ing.**

un·fin·ished [un fin'isht] **1** not finished; not complete: *unfinished homework.* **2** without some special finish; rough; not polished; not painted: *unfinished furniture. adj.*

un·i·sex [yü'nə seks'] having to do with, or designating clothing, hairstyles, etc. that are worn by members of both sexes. *adj.*

un·pack [un pak'] take out things packed in a box, trunk, etc: *to unpack one's clothes. v.*

un·til [un til'] · **1** up to the time of: *It was cold from December until April.* **2** before: *She did not leave until morning. prep.*

un·u·su·al [un yü'zhü əl] not in common use; not common; rare; beyond the ordinary: *We saw a very unusual lamp in the antique shop. adj.*

u·su·al [yü'zhü əl] in common use; customary; ordinary: *Snow is usual in most of Canada during winter. adj.*

V ▼▼▼

va·ca·tion [vā kā'shən] holidays: *She spent her vacation at the family cottage on Lake Erie. n.*

val·ley [val'ē] low land between hills or mountains: *Most large valleys have rivers running through them. n., pl.* **val·leys.**

> hat, āge, fär; let, ēqual, tėrm; it, īce; hot, ōpen, ôrder
> oil, out; cup, pùt, rüle; above, takən, pencəl, lemən, circəs
> ch, child; ng, long; sh, ship
> th, thin; ŦH, then; zh, measure

Van·cou·ver [van kü'vər] **1** an island of British Columbia, Canada, off the SW coast. **2** a seaport in SW British Columbia, opposite this island, on the Strait of Georgia.

vid·e·o [vid'ē ō'] **1** the visual part, as opposed to the sound, of a film or television program. **2** a recording of a movie or television program on a special tape to be played by a special machine. **3** having to do with images on a television or computer display. 1, 2 *n.*, 3 *adj.*
☛ *Etymology.* **Video** comes from the Latin word video, meaning '*I see*'.

vil·lage [vil'ij] a group of houses and other buildings, usually in a rural area, having fixed boundaries and some local powers of government. In Canada, a village is the smallest community that can have its own local government. *n.*

voice [vois] **1** the sound or sounds human beings make in speaking, singing, laughing, etc.: *The voices of the children could be heard coming from the playground.* **2** anything like speech or song: *the voice of the wind. n.*

voice mail [vois' māl'] **1** an automated answering system for telephone networks having touch tone, using a series of prerecorded prompts to which callers may respond by pressing the appropriate button to transfer them quickly and efficiently to the line they need. **2** a message or messages recorded on such a system. **3** a message recorded on any telephone answering machine. *n.*

vol·ley·ball [vol'ē bol'] **1** game played by two teams using a large ball and a high net. In volleyball, the players try to hit the ball with their hands so that it goes back and forth across the net without touching the ground. **2** the ball used in this game. *n.*

W ▼▼▼

wait [wāt] stay or stop doing something till someone comes or something happens: *Let's wait in the shade. v.*

warm [wôrm] **1** more hot than cold; having some heat; giving forth some heat: *a warm fire. She sat in the warm sunshine.* **2** make or become warm. **3** make or become cheered, interested, or friendly: *The speaker warmed to his subject. Her happiness warms my heart.* 1 *adj.*, 2, 3 *v.*

watch [woch]   **1** look carefully; observe closely: *The medical student watched while the surgeon performed the operation.*   **2** a device for telling time, small enough to be worn on the wrist or carried in a pocket.   **3** the time of duty of one part of a ship's crew: *A watch usually lasts four hours.*   1 *v.*, 2, 3 *n.*

wat·er·slide [wo'tər slīd']   usually a high slide, often with twists and turns and gentle bumps that ends in a pool and has water flowing down it.   *n.*

wave [wāv]   **1** move as waves do; move up and down or back and forth; sway: *The tall grass waved in the breeze.*   **2** signal or direct by waving: *The police officer waved the speeding driver to the side of the road.*   **3** a curve or series of curves: *My hair has waves, but my sister's hair is straight.*   1, 2 *v.*, 3 *n.*, **waved, wav·ing.**

wave pool [wāv' pül']   a pool with some device in it that creates waves.   *n.*

wear [wer]   have on the body: *He has to wear boots at work.*   *v.*, **wore, worn, wear·ing.**

weath·er [weTH'ər]   **1** the condition of the air with respect to temperature, moisture, cloudiness, etc.: *hot weather.*   **2** expose to the weather; wear or discolour by sun, rain, frost, etc.: *Wood turns grey if weathered for a long time.*   1 *n.*, 2 *v.*

Wednes·day [wenz'dā *or* wenz'dē]   the fourth day of the week, following Tuesday.   *n.*
☛ *Etymology.* **Wednesday** developed from Old English *Wōdnesdæg*, meaning 'day of Woden'; Woden, or Odin, was the chief Germanic god.

week·end [wēk'end']   **1** Saturday and Sunday as a time for recreation, visiting, etc.; the time between the end of one week of work or school and the beginning of the next: *a weekend in the country, Thanksgiving weekend.*   **2** spend a weekend: *They are weekending at the lake.*   1 *n.*, 2 *v.*

weren't [wėrnt]   were not.

where [wer *or* hwer]   in what place; at what place: *Where do you live?*   **2** to what place: *Where are you going?*   **3** from what place: *Where did you get that story?*   **4** the place or scene: *the when and the where of it.*   1–3 *adv.*, 4 *n.*

whisk·er [wis'kər *or* hwis'kər]   **1** Usually, **whiskers**, *pl.* the hair growing on a man's face, especially that on his cheeks and chin.   **2** a long, stiff hair growing near the mouth of a cat, rat, etc.   *n.*

whole [hōl]   **1** having all its parts; complete: *He gave us a whole set of dishes.*   **2** not injured or broken: *He came out of the fight with a whole skin.*   **3** in one piece: *The dog swallowed the meat whole.*   **4** well; healthy.   *adj.*

with·out [wiTH out' *or* with out']   **1** with no; not having; lacking; free from: *A cat walks without noise. She drinks tea without sugar.*   **2** outside of; beyond: *Soldiers were camped within and without the city walls.*   *prep.*

won·der·ful [wun'dər fəl]   causing wonder; marvellous; remarkable: *The explorer had wonderful adventures.*   *adj.*

work [wėrk]   **1** the effort of doing or making something: *It was hard work but she enjoyed it.*   **2** make, get, do, or bring about by effort: *The injured man worked his way across the room on his hands and knees.*   1 *n.*, 2 *v.*, **worked.**

worst [wėrst]   **1** most bad; of poorest quality: *None of them are good, but this one's the worst of the lot.*   **2** in the worst manner or degree: *He acts worst when he's tired.*   1 *adj.*, 2 *adv.*

writ·er [rī'tər]   a person who writes, especially one whose profession or business is writing, such as an author or journalist.   *n.*

writ·ing [rī'ting]   written form: *Put your ideas in writing.*   **2** something written; a letter, paper, document, etc.   *n.*

wrote [rōt]   the past tense of **write**: *She wrote her parents a long letter last week.*   *n.*

Y

yell [yel]   **1** cry out with a strong, loud sound: *He yelled with pain.*   **2** a special shout or cheer, especially one used by a school to encourage its sports teams.   1 *v.*, 2 *n.*

young [yung]   in the early part of life or growth; not old: *A puppy is a young dog.*   *adj.*, **young·er** [yung'gər], **young·est** [yung'gist].

youth [yüth]   **1** the fact or quality of being young: *She has the vigour of youth. He keeps his youth well.*   **2** the time between childhood and manhood or womanhood.   *n.*, *pl.* **youths** [yüths *or* yüTHz].